flowers chic & cheap

get happy

HERB TEA FOR LIFTING YOUR SPIRIT No.

Need an attitude adjustment? If the
gray and cloudy or your spirit could
little lift, there are lots of mood-enha
options out there. But few are as
delightful as sipping this caffeine-free
brew based on organic rooibos. Like
of sunshine, it begins to work its
magic as the bright flavors of lemon
and luscious peach do a tango on
tastebuds. Meanwhile, our carefully blend
blend of calming lemon balm, St. John's
and rhodiola does its part to help
blues away." So sip and smile, you
feeling peachy keen in no time.

The REPUBLIC of TEA

BE WELL RED' TEAS

Herbal Supplement · 36 Tea Bags · Net Wt 1.65

get relaxed.

HERB TEA FOR RELIEVING STRESS No.14

Stressed out and feeling kind of edgy? Join
the club. Ours is a fast-paced, demanding
world. The good news is this caffeine-free,
herbal blend delivers composure in a tea cup –
if only you'll take a moment to brew and sip.
The mood-mellowing begins instantly with
the calming aromas of lavender and rose
petals gently wafting up from the steaming
cup. Ahhhh. With each sip, a blissful blend of
health-promoting organic rooibos laced with
nerve-soothing chamomile and passionflower,
along with stress reducing eleuthero root and
helps you chill out, unbend and
Simply brew and breathe. Deep.

The REPUBLIC of TEA

BE WELL RED' TEAS

Herbal Supplement · 36 Tea Bags · Net Wt 1.65 oz (46.8g)

flowers
chic & cheap

arrangements with flowers
from the market or backyard

Carlos Mota

Photographs by William Waldron

Text by Rita Konig

Foreword by Margaret Russell

get
passionate.

HERB TEA FOR THE LIBIDO   No.17

YES! YES! YES! We all know that passion
makes the world go 'round. But we also know
it ebbs and flows. So when you feel the need
for a sensual nudge, make a date with this
caffeine-free herbal blend. Crafted from
organic rooibos, it includes exotic muira puama
bark and ashwagandha root, both said to
invigorate a lagging libido.* And, we've added
Peruvian maca root. Revered as an aphrodisiac,
let's just say it's popular for stimulating sexual
desires." On the lighter side, you'll detect a
flirty whiff of lemon verbena entwined with a
duo of passionflower and passionfruit. So go
ahead, light some candles, sip and get passionate.

The REPUBLIC of TEA

BE WELL RED® TEAS

Herbal Supplement · 36 Tea Bags · Net Wt 1.65 oz (46.8g)

Published in the United States by Clarkson Potter/
Publishers, an imprint of the Crown Publishing
Group, a division of Random House, Inc., New York.
www.crownpublishing.com
www.clarksonpotter.com

CLARKSON POTTER is a trademark and
POTTER with colophon is a registered trademark
of Random House, Inc.

Library of Congress Cataloging-in-Publication Data
Mota, Carlos, 1967–
Flowers chic & cheap : arrangements with flowers
from the market or backyard / Carlos Mota with Rita
Konig ; foreword by Margaret Russell. — 1st ed.
    p. cm.
1. Flower arrangement. I. Konig, Rita. II. Title.
  SB449.M68 2010
  745.92—dc22   2009036790

ISBN: 978-0-307-58798-5
Printed in China

Design by Marysarah Quinn

10 9 8 7 6 5 4 3 2 1

First Edition

Dedicated to Paul Siskin and
Perucho Valls

They are the reason I am in
this country. Thank you.

contents

Foreword by Margaret Russell 8
Introduction 10
Before You Get Started 12

less is more 14

more is more 86

brancholina 168

high & low 212

Bouquet Guide 270
Tools & Materials 276
Resources 280
Acknowledgments 284
Index 286

foreword

When I learned that my friend Carlos Mota, an editor at large at *Elle Decor,* was producing a book called *Flowers Chic & Cheap,* my first reaction was to laugh. It's true that Carlos is considered a master at artfully arranging flowers—and he is certainly admired for being deeply chic—but cheap? Never!

Carlos regularly zigzags the globe styling *Elle Decor* interiors and trendspotting for features, seemingly with scant regard for budget guidelines. But as the hundreds of sublime bouquets he has crafted for us over the past decade came to mind, I realized more funds went toward sustaining his devil-may-care life on the road than were invested in the glamorous flowers for our photo shoots. For Carlos is one of those rare stylists who can conjure unexpected magic by combining a fistful of leafy branches cut from a nearby tree with a standard-issue cylinder vase. And, as he shares his tips and reveals his secrets in this delightful book, now you can too.

Flowers are the most dramatic way to transform any humdrum room into a dazzling style statement. And long-standing so-called rules regarding scale, composition, and color can be ignored without concern; intuition and emotion should be your guide. Carlos's sassy pronouncements and clever, offbeat approach to working with flowers will surely educate and inspire you, and the results—captured in stunning images by celebrated photographer William Waldron—prove that anything from a take-out coffee cup to a teapot to a wastebasket can serve as a perfect container, beauty can be found in any blossom, and spontaneity is key. Carlos's no-nonsense, fashion-forward take on the extraordinary world of flowers is truly the ultimate in chic.

—Margaret Russell,

Editor in Chief, *Elle Decor*

introduction

I can't IMAGINE life without color or flowers. I am so glad that I was born after the Technicolor revolution. Don't get me wrong: some things are vastly improved in black and white, like hideous family pictures. But color is my passion, and I can't think of a better way to express that passion than through flowers. They make a room happy—and often change the look of it altogether.

I tend toward hot and spicy colors; it must be the Latin in me. I want flower arrangements that remind me of the sun, the beautiful beaches of Venezuela, parties in Caracas (now *that's* where you'll see the most beautiful flower decorations), the vibrant jungle, orchids, the rain, delicious fruit in every color, and the crystalline Caribbean. Everything in South America is so vivid and strong that I can see it even from my soothing lavender bedroom in New York. You won't be surprised to know that my motto is "White is not a color." For me, the only things that should be white are linens, towels, underpants, and, possibly, a wedding gown!

Though I love vivid and exotic colors, that doesn't mean I have hours to spend putting together fussy bouquets for my kitchen or bedroom. In fact, the simpler something is, the more I love it. So I've come up with quick methods for making beautiful yet uncomplicated arrangements. Here, I'll show you 100 ways to put together flower arrangements that are so simple to make, you will never need more than three different kinds of flowers—and most of them can be found at any flower store or even the supermarket or corner deli. Often the only effort you will need to invest is a quick trip to one of these places or just to your backyard to pick a simple rose or cut a branch. You will see how easy and simple it is to have flowers in your life every day. When you wake up in the morning, it's uplifting to have a sweet arrangement by your bed, or when you walk into your home after a terrible day, it's nice to be greeted by the splash of color from a few orchids. If you are having people over, make the effort to have that extra flower on the table.

Throughout, you'll run into many of my tricks, such as using herbs and branches to fill out an arrangement, grouping vases of similar shades together, and deconstructing those clumsy, inexpensive bouquets that you find already made up to create something really elegant. You'll learn my secret of "high low," where I put something tall next to something short, or mix expensive with cheap—simple compositions like these produce magical results. I like fancy English garden roses next to inexpensive pom-poms, and I find a little whimsical touch never hurts, such as using antique baby shoes as vases or adding a bird's nest to complete a wintry arrangement. But don't mix too many flower varieties. The strongest effects often come when you use just one kind of bloom. I love fabulous color combinations and playing off the shades in a room so that an arrangement works with the art in a room—or stands out as a work of art in itself. Most important, I will show you how significant the vessel you use is and how you can often find interesting vessels in the most unusual—or should I say usual—places. You'll think twice about throwing away beer bottles and tea tins!

Flowers are chic and beautiful on their own. Don't fuss with them. Don't be scared of them. After all, a glass of water with a single peony is as beautiful, and maybe even more so, than a tortured vase of ten. What's more, regardless of where you live these days, you can find nice flowers that are inexpensive, so there's really no excuse not to have them in your house, ALWAYS, even if it is just a single stem in your bathroom or living room.

I don't consider myself a flower expert; I can't even remember the names of most varieties! I just pick whatever is beautiful—usually a peony—and call it a day. On my frequent work travels styling rooms for magazines, one of the first things I do in a new place is go to the flower market or any interesting florist, or even the local museum for a visit to the Dutch and Flemish still life paintings. I always find inspiration somewhere.

So look around you, even when you are crazily running errands, and find inspiration. This book will give you quick instructions on how to make many arrangements. And, as is true of any "recipe," if you are missing a couple of ingredients, you can always create your own variation, whether by substituting a branch from your yard for flowers, or a soup can for a bottle. There are no rules. Once you learn how easy it is to throw together an elegant arrangement, you'll never want to live without one again.

before you
get started

1. Feed your flowers. If you don't have flower food (which you can get at a garden or flower store), use a clear, sugary soda like Sprite or 7UP—just a dash will do.

2. Before arranging your flowers, remember to tend to the stems so that they can drink: cut soft stems (like roses) at an angle and smash hard stems (like hydrangeas) with a hammer. The soft stems "heal" quickly, so cut them daily.

3. Use room temperature water, and throw a few pennies in the bottom of your vase or a drop of bleach in the water to prevent bacteria from taking over. And always make sure to remove any leaves, thorns, or other natural particles that promote bacterial growth.

4. Flowers do best in cool—but not cold—areas. Keep them away from radiators, air ducts, direct sunlight, poorly ventilated areas, and drafty doors. Mist them with clean water from time to time to keep them fresh.

5. Change the water in your vase every other day. Check to make sure that the stems are always submerged.

less

is more

salsa, baby, salsa!

You can find beautiful vases in the most unexpected containers, so keep your eyes peeled at the supermarket. Half the fun is finding the vase. I found these beautiful salsa jars and tea canisters at Whole Foods. I was drawn to the color of the labels. The salsa jars would be terrific for a Mexican lunch, tea containers would be charming for a tea party, and Campbell's soup cans filled with carnations would be fun for a dinner gathering.

1 pink peony

5 yellow English garden roses

2 white peonies

3 jars or cans with pretty labels

Cut the stems to be the same height as the jars or cans you are using. To get that randomly arranged casual look, vary the number of flowers and their colors among the vessels.

5 cacti

1 box of moss

5 high-gloss colored bowls

succulents

I can find beauty in the most unexpected places. I love to go to big stores and find beautiful cachepots, glassware, and baskets. I found these fabulous cacti at Home Depot and the colorful bowls at Pearl River in Manhattan's Chinatown. Combining the color and high gloss of the bowls with the rugged cacti transports them straight from the desert to the city.

5 cacti (I suggest an odd number, which makes the display feel less symmetrical and more playful.)

5 high-gloss colored bowls approximately 6 inches in diameter (Any bowl will do—even white would be chic.)

1 box of moss

Take a small cactus out of the plastic container, and place it in a bowl with its dirt.

Mold the moss by holding a large piece in your hands very tightly while forming it into a round shape.

Secure the cactus with the mounds of moss.

Repeat with remaining cacti and bowls.

Life is the flower for which love is the honey.

—VICTOR HUGO

spring bunny

This pretty still life moment is easy to reproduce, especially if you don't throw away any bottles. I just love the way these peonies are so truly open, but really, you can use any flowers, such as English garden roses, to make this composition because the humor is in the rabbit. It's great to use ornaments or knickknacks among flowers to complete a scene.

I ♥ NY

What else can I say about this iconic New York logo? I have been living in New York for many years, and I am crazy about the city. I found these paper coffee cups (see previous page) in a tourist store. I've seen ceramic mugs with the iconic heart in airports, but I love the humility of the paper cup. The image is clean and fresh, and the purity of the white peonies with the street style of the graphic is very cool. This arrangement will last about three days, but the cup may get a little soggy, so it's best to make it for a specific event: maybe to celebrate a friend's moving to New York or for a Woody Allen movie night?

Tissue paper

Glue

4 I ♥ NY paper cups (You can really use any paper cup. If you like blue and white, you could do this with some of the traditional coffee cups used in diners and coffee carts, or, for a child's birthday, you could do this with paper birthday party cups.)

2 perfect white peonies

Stuff a sheet of tissue paper between each cup, and put a dot of glue (such as Elmer's) at the bottom of each cup.

Fill the top cup one quarter full with water, just to cover the stem.

The weight of the water will keep the cups from falling, but you can add a couple of pebbles to the bottom cup if you're concerned about the cups' tipping over.

Cut the stems very short, so that they rest on the side of the cup and so the flower pops in the top cup. Even though the flowers are very close together, still cut the stems at slightly different lengths so that one is a little higher than the other, about a quarter of an inch difference.

I ♥ NY green mug

I love the bright green of this mug. How cute would it be to have one of these in front of each guest's place setting at a holiday party? Everyone can take the mug home as a party gift.

18 carnations

1 I ♥ NY green mug

5 green pom-pom carnations

Cut the carnations the same height as the mug. To make your bouquet, start by placing a single layer—six to eight—of carnations around the rim of the mug. Then add a second inner layer of carnations by resting more carnations on the first layer. Continue in this way until you have a dome of carnations, creating the effect of one large ruffle. Finally, add the pom-poms to the bouquet in random groups of three to five.

the sky is the limit

I am not a big fan of tulips. No matter what you do to them, they droop and flop around the vase. But I do like tulips when they are arranged in singles or pairs in bud vases.

Here, I have used French tulips, which I love for their unusually long stems. They are somewhat more rigid than ordinary tulips, and they take a winding route toward the sky, which gives them the appearance of free spirits.

With flowers like French tulips, it is good to remember you can use just one stem or a few stems since they are expensive and sold individually. They can cost $8 per stem, which sounds outrageous, but for $30 you can have as beautiful an arrangement as a vase full of a cheaper flower. This arrangement will look beautiful anywhere, but you could use a single arrangement of one stem in a vase, or you could place a group on a coffee table or make a row of them down a long dining room table.

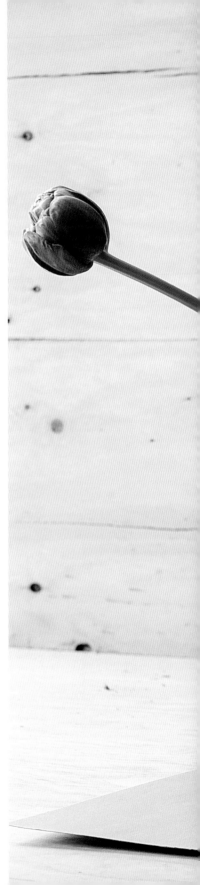

8 French tulips

6 different clear bottles (Mine are laboratory bottles—see the Resources section.)

1 sheet of art paper in a fun color

Varying the stem lengths gives this arrangement both grace and whimsy. For example, the tallest flower might be 18 inches, then a couple at 16 inches, one at 15 inches, two at 14 inches, and then—just to throw things off—one might be very short, as I did here, and put in a shot glass.

Place the bottles on a sheet of colored art paper. Choose your paper carefully because the color you pick will be reflected through the water in the bottles, which is a pretty effect.

thick moss or wheatgrass

beautiful tea or coffee cups

small, cut orchids

fancy a cuppa?

This arrangement looks like you had the florist do your flowers, but it's actually extremely simple. I love turning everyday and mundane items into little planters. You can put this arrangement just about anywhere in your home, but it would be really charming in front of each place at a dinner party with your guest's name hanging from the handle.

Small, cut orchids in beautiful colors (When cutting them, keep them shorter than 6 inches. Orchids come in an array of pretty colors, so choose the colors according to your china. If you have pastel-colored china, then use pastel flowers—the effect of which is springlike and relaxed. If your china is a deep primary color or patterned, then use the richer and deeper-colored flowers for a more dramatic and wintry look.)

1 bunch of orchids or sweet peas (or any small-scale flower)

Water tubes

Beautiful teacups or coffee cups (If you are making a plentiful arrangement, use matching cups and vary the color of the orchids. Alternatively, you could vary the cups and use matching orchids.)

Thick moss or wheatgrass

Cut your flowers double the height of the cups or mugs you are using.
Put them in the water tubes, with water.
Place the tubes in the cups, and add the moss to hold them in place.
THE END!

eggs over easy

I LOVE EGGS! In every shape and form, I just think the egg is one of the most beautifully designed natural objects. Of course, I love chickens, too!

I found these ostrich eggs in the produce section of a Whole Foods Market. Can you BELIEVE it? I thought you had to go to Africa to get these.

I've used orchids for this arrangement, but the eggs also look amazing with peonies, roses, or any small flower, really.

This arrangement is great to take to someone's house as a hostess gift, and, of course, it's perfect for an Easter party, but you don't have to wait until spring to bring it to the table.

2 ostrich eggs (If you can't find ostrich eggs, then any large eggs will do, such as goose or duck eggs.)

2 small orchids (no taller than 10 inches)

2 small water tubes, about 4 inches long

Moss

2 small terra-cotta pots—which remind me of egg cups

or

1 box filled with wheatgrass—which gives an outdoorsy feeling, as though the eggs are sitting in the grass

Crack the top of the eggs very carefully with a knife by tapping the side little by little as you go around. (Do this just as you would crack a boiled egg, but use a bigger knife and a harder tap. If you are feeling really adventurous, you can scramble the egg for breakfast!)

Wash the inside of the eggs with warm soapy water. (Sometimes you can find these eggs already empty and clean in fancy decorating stores.)

Put a few paper towels or moss (whichever you have plenty of) in the bottom of the eggs.

Cut the orchids and place them in the small water tubes.

Place the orchids inside the eggs and secure them with the moss, making sure that you don't see either the holes or the water tubes.

Then place the eggs in the two little terra-cotta pots or the wheatgrass box.

If you are using the wheatgrass box, you'll need to dig a small hole in the grass to hold the egg in place—just like in a nest.

cha cha cha

This is my Carmen Miranda moment. I found these crazy, colorful plastic bags at one of my ALL-TIME favorite shops in New York: Pearl River. But I bet you can find them in any party goods or Hallmark store. I love the explosion of colors—it's happy, fun. It's crazy! Because the bags are so colorful, I usually just fill them with greens. Here I used ferns, and every now and then, I put a poppy in the mix. To add more depth to the visual impact, use a fun tablecloth; here I used an Ikat.

Newspaper

12 to 15 stones

4 bags in four different colors

8 to 10 ferns, or any green foliage

1 to 3 large poppies

14 water tubes or 1 glass of water per bag

1 brightly colored or patterned tablecloth

Put a little newspaper and a few stones in the bottom of the bags to keep them open and weighted down, or put a large glass of water in each bag.

Making sure everything is either in a glass of water or in a water tube, place two to three ferns inside each bag, and arrange as you please. There are no rules here—just tuck them in whatever way looks right to you.

Then, place those perfect poppies.

1 perfect peony

1 clear glass bowl

1 tall glass cloche

pure beauty

The perfect peony, floating in the perfect bowl, trapped within a gleaming glass cloche, is not so much decor as a moment. It is very modern, and it would be beautiful on an all-white table with clean lines or on a mantelpiece.

Beauty is ethereal and eventually dies, and for me, that is what this beautiful peony represents. That is the beauty of this moment. Leave this arrangement until the last petal has fallen.

baby slippers

I found these beautiful antique baby slippers in Manhattan's Chinatown, but any baby shoes or silk slippers from an antiques shop or tag sale will do the trick for this arrangement. Using baby shoes is a fun idea for a baby shower or a little girl's birthday party. How about baby Converse sneakers filled with flowers "walking down the table"—how adorable would that be?

1 pair of tiny shoes

2 bunches of sweet william

Sweet william will last the length of the party without water, so just cut the stems very short and stuff them into the shoes.

Baby Jake

ALISON

fruit salad

This is the easiest and the simplest way to add color to a table. In most markets, ESPECIALLY country markets, fruit is sold in lovely little wooden boxes. Don't throw them away! Recycle them. They are even better looking if you leave them outside for a few days so the wood gets weathered.

If you have the space, run two long rows of eight boxes filled with various soft fruits down a long table. For an extra "natural" touch, go into the garden and gather some leaves to place in each corner of the boxes. The look is very country chic—a bit rustic and reminiscent of a day spent at the farmers' market. This arrangement would be perfect for a summer brunch— and it'll hold over the guests until the pancakes are ready!

ways to make your flowers last

Hybrid Delphinium have a hollow stem, so the water level in their vase needs to be high—all the way up the stem.

Hydrangea are hard to keep alive. Some varieties, such as Dutch White, don't live for more than a day or so. South American White are a hearty variety. They are usually a little off-white, but they dry and maintain their color well. The ones I bring home to dry usually keep their color for a year.

Orchids like warm, humid places. To re-hydrate a wilted orchid, soak the flower and stem in warm water. This doesn't always work but it can bring them back to life!

Peonies are stubborn! To get them to open, dip the heads in warm water. You can also help them along by peeling back the outer-most layer of petals. Then leave them in a humid room. I have even placed them in buckets and covered them with a garbage bag to make an artificial greenhouse.

Poppies absorb water through the little hairs on the stems, so you don't need to cut them. Just put them in very warm water. I always hand-peel closed poppies; this way I get them open and ready to use when I need them.

Roses must go immediately into water (or even cut them under water). If you wait too long to put them in water, air gets into the stem and travels up to the head, making them limp, even if the petals still look fresh.

Lilies need light to open. They close in the dark, and they like to be submerged in water. This is important to remember if you buy them for an evening party!

sushi to go

This is the traditional bento box that you find in any Chinatown or Asian market. But I think it makes a great centerpiece, and instead of using sushi, I used fruit. This could be very beautiful in a row of four for a wonderful Japanese dinner. It can also be lots of fun filled with candy if you are feeling more playful.

1 bento box

1 handful of each:
white cherries
white currents
black currents
red grapes
green figs
lychees

> I hate flowers. . . . I paint them because they are cheaper than models and they don't move.
>
> —GEORGIA O'KEEFE

less is more

Sometimes really simple things can make a big statement—for example, orchids (in this case, hybrid phalaenopsis) floating in bowls. Here I've used Japanese bowls, but small soup or condiment bowls from your kitchen will work as well. All you need is a very pretty flower floating in the bowl. These will look amazing scattered throughout the house or on a modern table with clean lines. It's very Asian looking—lots of them in perfect rows. DARLING, how chic!

artsy

I ADORE these very gourdlike and organic-looking vessels. They were designed by Gregory Kuharic, an American potter whose vases and ceramics are sold at Liz O'Brien on Fifth Avenue in New York. Sometimes all you need for an eye-catching arrangement are two or three sculptural vases with two perfect flowers. Here I have used two peonies, and though I haven't put flowers in the other two vases, they're still part of the arrangement. This is a great way to create a work of art for your home while still including the brightness of a few flowers.

Because the vases are in neutral colors, any flower with a punch of color will look great. In this case the arrangement feels very peaceful and tranquil, but see how easy it would be to make a stronger statement by adding a red book to the mix?

3 interesting vases or pots of
    different shapes and heights

2 large art books

2 beautiful, brightly colored
    flowers

Place your vases on two
books, in either neutral tones
or bright colors.
    Cut the stems of your two
flowers so that they are as
short as the smallest vase,
but remember not to cut both
flowers the same length—one
should be a little taller than
the other.
    Place them both in the
smallest vase.

THE IMPOSSIBLE COLLECTION   ASSOULINE

so fresh

Essentially this is a glass of water holding three azalea branches. You can substitute for the azaleas whatever flowers you have—roses, lilies, or peonies. What gives it fabulousness are the cake stands! If you don't have two, go buy another! But this does work with just one because even a little height adds some drama. The combination of the white flowers and the stands made of green milk glass makes this scene fresh and pretty. If you have only clear glass stands, use more-colorful flowers.

de-vine

Be ORGINAL! I am Latin and I love to make statements, so when I found this beautiful beat-up old birdcage, I wanted to use it for a whimsical centerpiece. To give this elderly birdcage a modern twist, I added a stark white vase and those fabulous hot pink orchids. It would look great with a silver vase, too. The important thing is to use a sharp and bright color to balance the dark cage.

The real joy here is the crazy climbing vine. Use real ivy, if you can. You'll want to put it in water tubes and hide the tubes within the moss inside the cage.

1 white or silver vase

1 birdcage

2 cut orchids

8 clumps of moss

About 2 yards of vine such
  as ivy

Place the vase in the center of the cage with two orchids in it. Make sure that one orchid is shorter than the other.

Pop the moss around the vase and even outside the cage if you like.

Next, delicately wrap the vine up the cage and through the cage's bars.

Tip: Use small pieces of wire to hold the vine in place. If you are very careful, you might be able to forego the wire by twisting the ivy through the bars of the cage.

Where flowers degenerate man cannot live.

—NAPOLEON

life imitates art

I like taking the color from a painting or a photograph and reflecting it in a flower arrangement. With the example at right, the minimal maple leaves almost disappear, giving the painting a newfound depth. You can do this with almost any piece of art. In the image at left, the opposite is true because rather than blending into the painting, the orange roses actually act as an accessory to the painting. Find a style moment in your house that you want to enhance—if not a painting, then a sculpture or an uphol-stered chair. You'll find this great fun, and it'll force you to really take a second look at your home and decor.

the perfect moment

We are used to seeing lilies arranged in bunches of at least twelve or more. Guess what? It is not necessary. There is nothing more divine than four or five lilies in either bud or small vases displayed throughout the house. I found this pretty deep red lily at my corner deli. I was looking, particularly, for deep red to match both the painting and the red vase, and I found it! I created the perfect moment with almost nothing.

1 lily stem with a few flowers

1 small Chinese vase

Just cut the stem so that the lily stem stands about 22 inches at the highest point.

I perhaps owe having become a painter to flowers.

—CLAUDE MONET

my name is Hermes

I love this boy! Hermes, messenger of the gods, is immortalized by KPM (Königliche Porzellan-Manufaktur Berlin) with this eighteenth-century statue. This is a tricky one because, like the garlands on page 255, I didn't make this garland. I found it at the flower market in New York City and couldn't resist it. But I have included it in this book because, should you come across any flower garlands, I think this is a fun way to use them. They are fabulous thrown over almost anything—a lamp, your mantel, a mirror, or for a special occasion. If you are feeling adventurous, you could use them as the tiebacks for your draperies!

deli delicious

How often have you received one of those HEEEDIOUS bouquets bought from a corner deli or supermarket? I am a great believer in finding beauty everywhere, so I decided to deconstruct the boring mishmash bouquets found at every flower stand and make something elegant out of them.

Separate every flower by type and color. That will give you an idea of what you have to play with.

Once you have laid out the flowers, group them by style or shape. In my bunch I grouped together all the different-colored chrysanthemums and the purple and green pom-poms, because unlike the sunflowers or the stocks, the similar shapes of the chrysanthemums make them work well together. The tighter the arrangement, the better they look. This style is very French.

Make small and tight bouquets with the flowers, and pop them into little silver cups or small metal buckets. This will look charming and very country, as if you went into your garden and picked flowers. Use them on a table at an outdoor lunch. They are also lovely beside a bed.

Arrange the remaining single stems, which will vary greatly, individually in bud vases.

If you have two sunflowers, then stand them in a tall black narrow vase—this will look wonderful. Most of the time, a single-stem flower in a clear, simple little bottle is just beautiful. As you can see in the photograph at left, I have put one iris in a bud vase. You get such a random assortment of flowers in these types of bouquets that one bunch of flowers can be used throughout your house.

In the case of the baby's breath, which is often the first to be thrown away because we think of it as just florist's filler, look how pretty, delicate, and modern it is on its own. The baby's breath arrangement, opposite, would look beautiful on a dressing table or vanity, or in the bathroom.

all Carlos!

I found these graphic coffee mugs at Bed Bath & Beyond. How fun would it be to throw a birthday party for your best friend or significant other and place his or her name all over the house, on top of the mantel, or along the dining room table like this? You could also spell things like "Kiss me" or "I love you"!

Here I have used red dahlias because I think the color works beautifully against the white ceramic and the black letters, but you can use any flower you want.

green tea

I love ANYTHING overscaled! Which is why I like these White King Protea—they are big and a bit strange. But the stars of this show are really the vases: two glass cylinders, about 12 inches and 18 inches high, that I wrapped in Japanese rice paper. Wrapping a cylindrical vase is so simple, and it turns a very ordinary glass into an unusual and beautiful vessel. Plus, the stylistic opportunities are huge because you can wrap just about anything around your vase, such as old book pages, *Vogue* covers, Chinese newspapers, or beautiful wrapping paper. Choose your flowers to go with the paper you have selected for the vase.

To wrap your cylinders, measure the height of the vase and cut your paper accordingly.

Run a strip of double-sided tape down the length of one vertical end of the paper.

Stick the taped edge of the paper to the vase; then wrap the paper around the vase and secure it with another strip of double-sided tape.

nice bud!

Bud vases are so useful to have in bulk at home. I think they look best displayed in an assortment of colors as a collection. I especially love the ones that come in fabulous glazes—mine are made by a company called Middle Kingdom, but you can find glazed ceramics at most home stores or through on-line wholesalers. Vibrant colors and simple shapes look beautiful pretty much anywhere, whether you use one, two, or ten.

Here I have used peonies, but since each vase will hold only one flower, it really can be anything. You know when you go to the flower shop and see those beautiful roses for $10 a stem and you think you could never afford them? Well, think again! A bud vase is the ideal vessel for those incredibly expensive and perfectly beautiful flowers. Place one in a bud vase and put it by your bed. It will look as magnificent as three dozen.

Say it with flowers.

—PATRICK F. O'KEEFE

1 small bamboo steamer

1 small chunk of moss

3 orchids

steamed dumplings

You will be surprised by the endless possibilities for centerpieces that you can find in a Chinese market. I found this bamboo dumpling steamer at Pearl River in Manhattan's Chinatown, but you can get these steamers at any Asian market. I think it is just the chicest thing to have one of these arrangements in front of each plate at a dinner party. It is minimal and simple, but it is a very sophisticated, worldly look.

3 orchids

1 small water tube filled with water

1 small bamboo steamer

1 small chunk of moss

Place your orchids in the water tube.
  Then pop them in your bamboo steamer and anchor them in place with the moss.

In this world
we walk on the roof of hell
gazing at flowers.

—KOBAYASHI ISSA

orange for fall

I have accumulated bottles in just about every shade, but I especially love using my orange and yellow ones in the fall. This design would make a fabulous centerpiece for a cozy autumn dinner or for Thanksgiving.

To add texture and surprise, I love to throw seasonal fruits like small pumpkins (I HATE hauling the big ones home), apricots, or pomegranates around the vases.

Sometimes I use flowers simply to adorn a still life moment rather than for creating a conventional flower arrangement. This simple orchid adds beauty and color to the scene, but the rest of the pots are so beautiful they don't need anything added to them, and it would be a great shame to remove the lids. Because I am crazy about orchids, I used one here for an exotic touch, but you can use whatever you like. Just make sure that the flower you choose is in the same color group as the bottles.

about 5 stems of mint

2 tall Perrier bottles

3 shorter
beer bottles

about 8
rosemary
branches

after party

This arrangement is made up entirely of herbs and recycled Perrier and beer bottles from last night's party, but you can do this with any bottles that come in good colors. Personally, I love this fabulous emerald green.

Once you have taken the labels off your bottles, which you can do by soaking them in hot water until the label and glue easily scrub off, you need a few beautiful herbs, either from the garden or the supermarket. I love the monotone look here, and to achieve it, I used rosemary and mint. Not only does this arrangement look beautiful but it smells delicious, too.

This makes sense in a kitchen, of course, but that is not the only place for this decoration. A row of three on your mantel or in your bathroom, where the scent will really be appreciated, would be wonderful.

About 5 stems of mint

About 8 rosemary branches

2 tall Perrier bottles

3 shorter beer bottles

Randomly divide the mint and the rosemary among the bottles, keeping the lengths somewhat the same.

There are no rules here: use two stems of rosemary in one vase, mix rosemary and mint in another. What is important is to keep the arrangement high, so the herbs should be twice as tall as the Perrier bottles. Make sure that the branches go in both directions so you get that pretty V shape rather than having them look as though they are blowing in the same direction!

more

is more

French bouquet

This is the most traditional French bouquet—you can find bouquets like it at almost every corner flower stand in Paris. Basically, it is a combination of multicolored roses tied together. But I didn't go to Paris for this. I found the ingredients next to the oranges and cut-up melon at a corner market near my apartment. The market was already selling small bunches of ten roses, so I bought three bunches, removed the leaves, and bundled them together to make a more generous arrangement. This is so easy: you can do it by buying six or eight bunches of different-colored roses and tying them together.

Most of the time I like to use a ceramic vase so that you don't see the stems. Choose a bright color. Here you can see how the contrasting turquoise makes these brightly colored roses pop.

2 to 3 dozen roses in different colors (The best colors to mix are red, yellow, orange, hot pink, and sugar pink.)

Florist's tape

Make sure your roses are open.

Clean the stems by removing the leaves. Sometimes it is nice to keep one or two leaves near the bloom in the bunch.

To start the bunch, take one stem and add three stems to it to make a minibouquet. Then add five stems around the bouquet. Then seven, then nine, and so on, until you run out of roses and end up with a lush, full bouquet.

To get that beautiful dome shape, keep the first flower at the top and in the center of the bunch, and add each additional flower a little lower than the previous flower.

When you have finished, tie the bunch with florist's tape, and cut the stems so that they are all the same length. Slice the stems in two so the roses can drink. The more roses you have, the better this bouquet looks, so keep this arrangement in mind the next time you find inexpensive, ordinary roses at the grocery store or corner market.

shopping, anyone?

Don't throw away those beautiful bags after a shopping spree. Of course, some of them are nicer than the others, but those Hermès bags with that lovely signature orange OR the sweet lavender Bergdorf Goodman bags are too good to toss! Or if you've been disciplined and haven't shopped in a while, you can go to any stationery store and find a shopping bag with a great color and pattern. That's the fun of this.

1 good-looking shopping bag

Tissue paper or newspaper

1 tall glass of water

1 dozen soft pink peonies

2 to 3 hot pink peonies

Stuff the bottom of the bag with some tissue paper or newspaper so that it stays open.

Fill a glass that is about the same height as the bag with water, and start adding the soft pink peonies to make a bouquet (see Bouquet Guide on page 270).

Once you have made your bouquet, add the hot pink peonies in random spots to create a polka-dot look.

This arrangement makes a great gift, but it's also fabulous lining the steps up to a porch or a path to a tent for a summer party. For those, I might even forego the fancy shopping bags and just use brown paper ones!

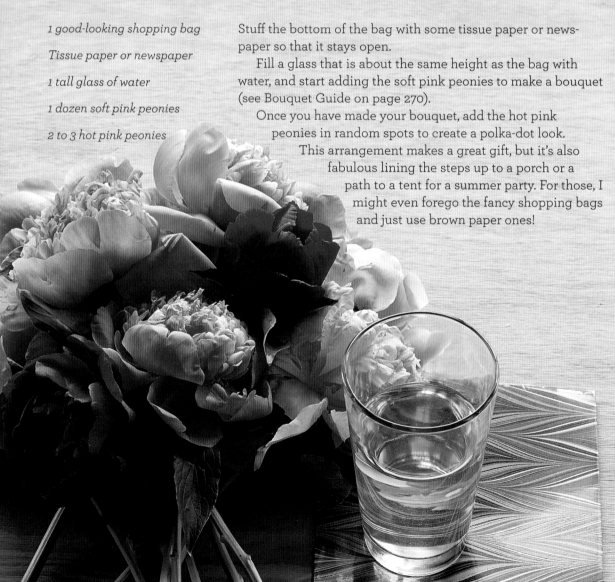

let's paint the town

I LOVE the simplicity of these paint cans. You can buy them in any hardware or paint store—I got mine at Home Depot. Even though they are paint cans, they are silver and shiny, which makes them look modern. If you are lucky enough to have a collection of cans with beautiful colors dripping down the side, you have ideal vases! Given the simple form of paint cans, you can use pretty much any flowers in these containers. I used peonies and roses here.

I love how the colors bounce from soft pink to medium to dark. To create that effect, mix flowers of three different shades. To get that POP, add four white peonies randomly on one side of the largest arrangement. This "imperfection" gives it some character. You can add the three flowers randomly to any one of the arrangements and the effect will be the same.

You don't have to keep all three cans together; you can spread them throughout the house. The big can would make a great centerpiece for a dinner party.

3 paint cans in a variety
of sizes

Large Can
12 soft pink peonies
4 white peonies

Medium Can
2 dozen hot pink English
garden roses

Small Can
3 dark red peonies

Large Can: Make your bouquet, and then add four white peonies to the right-hand side of the bouquet.

Medium Can: Make your bouquet with the hot pink English roses.

Small Can : Cut the three dark red peonies, and pop them into the can—they require very little arranging. Keep two of the stems a similar height, about an inch taller than the can, and make the third one 2 inches taller than the can.

For fun, leave a couple of the can lids on the table.

lunch is served

There is nothing more satisfying than a delicious bowl of soup. So open your kitchen cabinet and take out your soup tureen and fill it with anemones! And season with humor (as important an ingredient as salt) by adding a large spoon! This is a great centerpiece for lunch or dinner.

You can also use roses, peonies, or carnations instead of anemones.

1 block of oasis, cut to fit the bottom of the soup tureen

1 soup tureen

2 dozen soft pink anemones

1 dozen blue anemones

½ dozen amethyst anemones

1 large spoon

1 purple table runner

Submerge the oasis in water for about 5 minutes.

Fill the tureen half full with water.

Place the soaked oasis block in the bottom of the tureen.

Cut the stems of the flowers about three quarters of the height of the soup tureen (so if the tureen were 8 inches, you would cut your flowers to 6 inches).

Start with the largest amount of anemones, in this case the pink ones, and create a domelike shape. Then randomly (in bunches of two or three) add the purple and amethyst flowers in the remaining space.

Place the spoon at an angle, anchoring it in the oasis.

rustic artichokes

I love the shape, color, and flavor of artichokes. This arrangement gives you two for the price of one—you can use the artichokes in this centerpiece, and when the party's over, you can roast them! For a little unexpected surprise, I have added fiddlehead ferns, which I LOVE, and green berries.

I would use this arrangement on the table for a summer lunch on the terrace.

About 15 small artichokes

3 old rustic pots—and if they have dirt on them, so much the better

1 small bunch of green berries, which you can find in the deli

About 10 small fiddlehead ferns

Group the artichokes in fours or fives (whatever fits).

Cut the stems so that they can sit in the pots.

Cut the green berry branches very short so that you end up with about twelve much smaller bunches.

Add the berries to the artichokes where you see holes.

Last, BUT NOT LEAST, add in the ferns for height so that they move slightly in the breeze.

True friendship is like a rose: we don't realize its beauty until it fades.

—EVELYN LOEB

haute reading

I love putting things on pedestals, from people to flowers. Using books to elevate an arrangement is one of my favorite tricks and a trademark in my photo shoots. The vase here is only 10 inches, but when it's on a table on top of books, the arrangement has much more importance.

The first thing I do when I buy a book is to remove the dust jacket to reveal the beautiful linen binding. I group the books by color for a greater impact, pulling together flowers a shade that complements the color of the book. For drama, I create a monochromatic look, like the one with the red carnations to the left and the arrangement of hot pink peonies and orangey-red-pink books on pages 102–103.

For a softer look, I use a quieter palette, such as the light blues, gentle pink roses, and touches of mint on the next page. This is perfect for spring.

I think the book trick works best on either a coffee table or an end table and sometimes in the middle of a bookcase.

Vase

2 dozen carnations to match your books

8 sprigs of mint

6 to 8 books, all in the same color and stacked by size

Start with the first ring of carnations, which should be cut the same length as the vase.

Then add the second inner ring, about an inch taller, and carry on until you have created a dome filling the vase.

When the bouquet is complete, take the mint and add the sprigs randomly throughout the bouquet. Place the books where you'd like to show off your bouquet and set the vase on top.

Surrealism: Two Private Eyes
Surrealism: Two Private Eyes 1
JACK PIERSON
All of a sudden

INSIDER'S PARIS

MARIE ANTOINETTE · THE JOURNEY · ANTONIA FRASER · NAN A. TALESE DOUBLEDAY

ANGELS
AN ENDANGERED SPECIES · MALCOLM GODWIN

DAVID HICKS: DESIGNER · ASHLEY HICKS

POOLE POTTERY · HAYWARD & ATTERBURY

5 medium to large stems of
purple hydrangeas

a beautiful colored-glass pitcher

about 5 small bunches of lilacs

some pretty floral tape

summer lilacs

Purple and green is one of my favorite color combinations. And I love lilacs. When you start to see them in the market, you know spring is here. I especially adore the way the lavender in the lilacs looks mixed with this crisp, clean green water pitcher. This is an extremely versatile summer look, and it would be beautiful anywhere outdoors—for a lunch on the terrace or even up on the kitchen counter, or placed on the dresser in a bedroom where the fresh scent of lilacs will gently permeate the room.

5 medium to large stems of
*   purple hydrangeas*

About 5 small bunches of lilacs

A beautiful colored-glass
*   pitcher (Green works best.)*

Twine

With a hammer, smash the bottom inch of the stems of both the hydrangeas and the lilacs. This allows them to drink!

Cut the first four stems the same height as the water pitcher. The fifth branch should be about 2 inches taller than the others (this may vary between plants, but essentially you want the bottom of the bloom on this one to come to the top of the others). Place it in the center of the arrangement.

Place the hydrangeas in the pitcher first, from left to right, so they lean against the side of the pitcher.

Cut the stems of the five lilac branches to be the same length as the vase, tie them together with twine, and then literally stick them in on one side of the bouquet.

Earth laughs in flowers.

—RALPH WALDO EMERSON

1 colorful ceramic vase

1 wooden box

12 chartreuse roses

sweet and sour

I love the sweetness and the softness of this pink English garden rose against the acidity of the tighter chartreuse roses. The vase is a particularly important part of this arrangement. It has a simple, ordinary shape, but the strong color of the apple-y yellow/green ceramic pops fabulously against the other two colors. I like ceramic vases; the glazes are beautiful and the ceramic masks any unsightly stems and, even worse, dirty water.

18 big English garden roses

In joy or sadness, flowers are our constant friends.

—KAZUKO OKAKURA

About 18 big English garden roses

About 12 chartreuse roses

1 colorful ceramic vase

1 wooden or other type of box to use as a pedestal

Make sure that your garden roses are fully open.

Make your bouquet as shown on pages 271–273.

Then, randomly, and in groups of three or four, add the chartreuse roses into the arrangement in the holes left between the roses.

If I have extra flowers, I like to take apart the buds very carefully and leave the petals at the base of the vase. This extends the arrangement, giving it some softness and depth. But this is optional—fun for a dinner or an event, less so if you are just doing it for yourself, because the petals will dry up quickly.

To pull a rose apart without bruising or ripping the petals, hold the stem in one hand, take the head in your other hand, and with your fingers quite tightly around the head, turn the rose like a dial counterclockwise until it pulls away from the stem. It will still look beautiful, falling apart without losing its shape.

water me

If you look around your house, you are sure to find everyday vessels that can be used as vases. I found this delightful watering can at Home Depot in a fabulous chartreuse color (I KNOW! I LOVE chartreuse, and it is a very trendy color).

This would be DIVINE for an outdoor wedding. Imagine a beautiful apple green tablecloth with this arrangement at the center, combined with garden trugs and tools—very humble, very Marie Antoinette, DARLING!

Here I used peonies, white daisies, and rosemary. But this could be done in a more loose, English style with wildflowers from your garden.

1 large watering can (It could be an old one, too; as long as it isn't plastic, it will look great.)

1 dozen white peonies

About 1 dozen daisies or scabious

About 15 stems of rosemary

Cut all but three of the peonies about the same height as the watering can, so that they sit at the mouth of the can.

Cut the remaining three about two-thirds of an inch longer to create that crazy tail effect in the back of the can.

Put the short ones in the front and the longer ones behind.

To add a rustic, just-came-in-from-the-garden feel, stick the rosemary behind the peonies and on one side of the can, so that it looks as though you are framing the peonies, almost like a peacock fanning its feathers.

When the bouquet is finished, randomly add in a few of the small white flowers, but that is totally optional.

For that extra surreal touch and to create an homage to nature, I add moss and those little rosemary leaves to the base of the watering can when it is in place.

hot and spicy

I found this colorful selection of pots at Wal-Mart. This idea was inspired by arrangements I saw at the Union Square Greenmarket in New York City; I decided to use dried flowers in this instance because fresh flowers are wet and would just ruin the paper. To fill the pots, I chose lavender, dried chilies, and gomphrena, but these are just pots, after all. You can really fill them with anything you want. Imagine them overflowing with fruits or vegetables, for example?

Art is the unceasing effort to compete with the beauty of flowers and never succeeding.

—MARC CHAGALL

6 sheets of 12-inch-square paper (I used gift wrap) cut in half on the diagonal so you are left with 2 triangles per sheet

4 large bunches of large dried chili peppers

3 bunches of lavender

4 bunches of gomphrena

1 small cactus rose

3 medium pots

2 large pots

1 small pot

Twine

Group the chili peppers in three big bunches.

Place each chili pepper bunch at one acute edge of the paper triangle with the ends of the stems running along the bottom of the triangle and the chili pepper facing the triangle's point.

Then roll the chili peppers in the paper.

Secure the bunch with some packing twine; then fold back the excess paper at the top to reveal the chili peppers.

Continue this procedure with the rest of the dried flowers, and place two to three arrangements in each of the medium and large pots. Plant the cactus in a little pot with planting soil.

6 sheets of 12-inch-square paper

2 large pots

4 bunches of gomphrena

1 small pot

cream of roses

This is my traditional, Ralph Lauren moment! I found this beautiful blue-and-white soup tureen at my friend's house. Filled with a wonderful combination of deep, rich-colored roses, it feels quintessentially English to me. So when someone gives you one of those dreadful store-bought bouquets or when you go to the corner deli and find they have only orange and red roses left, HERE'S what you do: deconstruct the bouquet to create something beautiful and worthy of display. The key here is not to mix more than two colors and *to arrange them in clumps;* don't disperse them evenly. This is a fabulous holiday look.

1 block of oasis, cut to fit the bottom of the soup tureen

1 soup tureen

About 2 dozen fully open orange roses

About 2 dozen fully open deep red roses

Submerge the oasis in water for about 5 minutes.

Make sure your roses are as wide open as possible. To do so, you can put them in warm water or blow them gently with a blow dryer.

Place the oasis in the bottom of the tureen.

Fill the tureen halfway with water.

Cut approximately eight orange roses about the same length as the height of the soup tureen, to go around the outside.

Next, keep placing roses around the tureen, working inward and adding an inch or two to the length of each rose as you go, until you get to the middle.

After you have finished with the orange roses, randomly add the red ones in groups of three. The stems of the red roses should be the same length as the height of the tureen.

Place the red roses wherever you see holes in the bouquet and wherever the bouquet feels lacking. I usually place them on the left and the right sides of the bouquet.

Make sure that the random clumps of red do not touch, because the colors should appear quite chunky.

you've got a delivery

These delicious plastic take-out containers come in all colors and sizes, and I think they are JUST PLAIN CUTE for a wedding or lunch, or even to take as a gift to someone's house. I enjoy filling them with a favorite flower of mine: carnations. They're fun and sort of kitschy, and that's the point you're making with this arrangement.

*6 or more (the more the merrier)
take-out containers*

*12 dozen carnations (Don't
worry, they are cheap!)*

Make sure that you can put water in your take-out containers. If
you can't, then a glass of water will do the trick.

Group the carnations in as big bunches as possible. What
makes these carnations such heaven is that when they are
packed so tightly together, they just become one big ruffle.

Tie each bunch with a rubber band or florist's tape. Then cut
the stems a little bit shorter than the height of the container so
that when you put them in the container or glass, the blooms sit
right on top of the container's edge.

Again, the more you use, the better.

quiet moment

I love this corner in my friend's house; it is so peaceful and quiet. Basically the key to this scene is the beautiful water pitcher: that fabulous turquoise glaze just pops out against the bamboo furniture. I used very soft pale pink and green hydrangeas. The wonderful thing about these flowers is that whether you use two or six, they always look fabulous due to their density and shape.

6 stems of hydrangeas

1 ceramic pitcher in a beautiful color

Cut four stems about the same height as the pitcher, but keep the lengths a little uneven.

Smash the bottoms of the stems so they can drink tons of water.

Place the four stems around the outside of the pitcher.

Take the last two hydrangeas and cut them a little taller than the others. Place them on top of the others.

BASTA.

Get out your favorite Jane Austen novel.

Where flowers bloom so does hope.

—LADY BIRD JOHNSON

sunburst

I bought these chrysanthemums in my favorite colors—lavender and purple—at the corner deli. I love the spikiness of the petals, which reminds me of the spikes in this metal sun sculpture. The book gives the flowers a stage on which to shine.

About 8 lavender chrysanthemums

About 8 purple chrysanthemums

1 square glass vase

1 thick book in a neutral color

Cut all stems 1 to 2 inches shorter than the vase.

Add the first ring of lavender chrysanthemums, resting them on the side of the vase.

Next, add a second inner ring to the vase, and continue with a third and fourth ring until you have completed your bouquet. Then randomly add the darker chrysanthemums in groups of three to five.

Display on top of the book.

Flowers seem intended for the solace of ordinary humanity.

—JOHN RUSKIN

royal china

How chic is this little bouquet? Imagine eight of them down a long table with a red silk tablecloth. The chrysanthemums and the beautiful red lacquer are strong Chinese symbols that remind me of Imperial China.

5 white chrysanthemums

4 yellow chrysanthemums

20 yellow pom-poms such as Craspedia (also known as Billie Balls)

Florist's tape or a rubber band

1 silver beaker 4 or 5 inches tall

Group the five white chrysanthemums together in your hand.

Then add two yellow ones on one side and two on the other side.

Tie them together with a rubber band or florist's tape.

Cut the stems a half inch shorter than the silver cup.

At the very end, add the Billie Ball pom-poms in groups of three at the points where the yellow and white chrysanthemums meet.

it's so me

This particular bouquet SCREAMS Carlos Mota for two reasons: one, it uses a palette of hot pink and chartreuse, and two, it combines expensive English garden roses with really cheap green chrysanthemums from the deli.

When I see this bouquet, I smile and feel like I want to dance; it's a very happy bunch.

About 2 dozen hot pink English garden roses

About 2 dozen Kermit green pom-poms (Santini chrysanthemums)

1 medium, blue, modern ceramic vase

Make sure that your flowers are fully open and make a bouquet following the guide on pages 271–273.

After you've filled in the holes, add, randomly and in groups of two and three, the green pom-poms for that playful and whimsical effect.

j'adore

I loved the tranquillity of this room, but it needed some color! Nothing too loud or exuberant, however, which is why these very pretty peonies in pale green and pink were the perfect thing. They added the touch of color I was looking for but in a very subdued way, and the turquoise of the vase offered a helpful little punch too! In fact, this is a very useful vase: you would not necessarily imagine that such a strong color would be a great neutral, but the shape is versatile. I recommend having at least one statement vase like this in your cupboard.

6 pink peonies

3 green peonies

1 ceramic vase in a bright color

Cut the pink peonies a little shorter than the vase so that their petals will rest on the vase's lip.

Place the pink peonies around the edge of the vase, leaving a hole in the middle.

Cut the green peonies about half an inch taller than the vase, and place them in the center, filling the void. The color contrast of the peonies may seem subtle, but the effect is like pinning a beautiful Van Cleef broach to a dress.

Miss Havisham

I love color, but there is always an exception—even to one's own rules. When I saw these velvety silver leaves (dusty miller) at the market, I thought they were just beautiful—so much so that I was inspired to make a silver and white arrangement. It is so nostalgic, dreamy, and wintry, don't you think? We took this photograph on a rainy afternoon, and I love the wistful feeling that it captured. But interestingly, if you took this arrangement outside on a summer day, for a wedding or a christening, it would be a much more vibrant and cheerful-looking bouquet.

2 dozen silver dusty miller

6 to 8 white scabiosas (the flowers)

3 Lysimachia (the pointy things)

Start with the main bouquet of the silver leaves (see pages 271–273 for the bouquet).

Then, in the center of the bouquet, randomly add the scabiosas.

Last, place the three pointy *Lysimachia* in the top of the bouquet.

real or fake?
that is the question!

I think that everything in this picture is perfect. This is my own nightstand, and all the little objects on it are presents from dear, dear friends. As for the flowers, well, they are just beautiful: the color, the scale, and the fact that they are opened just perfectly. But can you tell if they are real or not? I will leave that up to you.

Don't be scared of silk flowers. If they are arranged properly, they can look just as beautiful as the real things.

About 1 dozen soft pink peonies

3 hot pink peonies

6 chartreuse ranunculuses

1 short ceramic vase

Florist's tape

Group all the soft pink peonies together (see Bouquet Guide on pages 271–273).

Then randomly add the three hot pink peonies, followed by the six green ranunculuses.

Tie them all together with florist's tape, and cut them shorter than the vase so that they sit on the edge of it.

Flowers are love's truest language.

—PARK BENJAMIN

color is the answer

I am a great believer in consistency; to me, that is the basis of style. The basis of my style is color and orchids. In a corner of my living room, I placed two vases of orchids in spicy colors. In front of the sofa I mixed two shades of the same vanda orchid, and next to the sofa, the same variety in a different color and arranged to look taller.

2 dozen pink vanda orchids

2 dozen purple vanda orchids

2 dozen orange vanda orchids

1 short ceramic vase (about 6 inches tall)

1 taller ceramic vase (about 12 inches tall)

Florist's tape

For the Shorter Vase: Mix the two colors of orchids together by essentially taking one purple flower and then one pink flower and working your way through the bouquet alternating between the two colors.

When you finish the bouquet, tie the stems with florist's tape and cut them a little shorter than your vase so that they're hidden by the edge of the vase.

For the Taller Vase: Tie the stems as above to make your bouquet, and cut them to about 8 inches.

As you can see, aqua or turquoise vases work fabulously with these hot-colored orchids.

nine to five

This is my little corner office at home, and this arrangement is dead simple. It involved a trip around the corner for two bunches of yellow James Storey orchids. I love how each of these sunny, yellow stems takes its own route. It makes for a very airy and playful arrangement.

2 dozen James Storey orchids

1 tall, narrow colored-glass vase (about 16 inches tall)

Take the flowers out of the plastic and cut the stems, varying the lengths.

Then just stuff them in! They will find their own direction, creating a sunburst effect.

Imagination is more important than knowledge.
—ALBERT EINSTEIN

color

Don't be afraid of color! Take a color that you like and explore all the variations. I love purple and lavender.

Mix and match; for example, a blue vase is great with either purple or yellow flowers. A green vase will look great with hot pink flowers. A pink vase will be fabulous with white flowers.

Don't mix more than two colors together, unless they are part of the same family.

If you feel daring and add another color, make sure it is one with a lot of contrast.

Look through your house and pick a color, whether in a pillow, a piece of art or a lampshade, and create a bouquet to match it.

I prefer colored glass or ceramic vases to clear glass because having a color enhances the flowers and it also hides the dirty water!

In the winter I tend to go for stronger, more jewel-toned colors: deep purples and reds, and flowers like black roses and catleyas in dark colors.

In the summer I like to have spicy colors and bright colors: orange, yellows, pinks—I am not a big fan of pastel colors.

Break the rules! For example, it is such a cliché to use white and blue flowers for the summer.

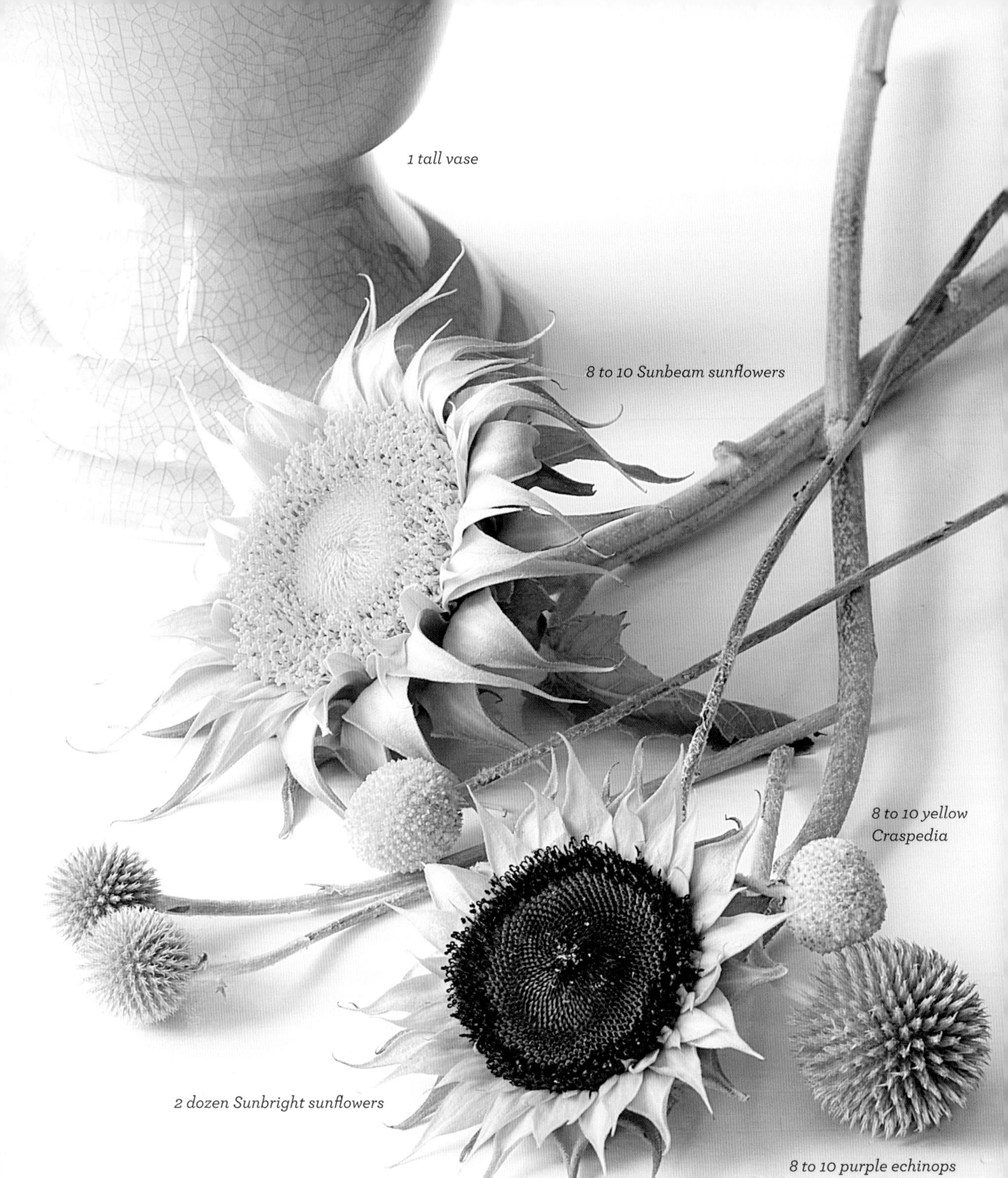

1 tall vase

8 to 10 Sunbeam sunflowers

8 to 10 yellow
Craspedia

2 dozen Sunbright sunflowers

8 to 10 purple echinops

better than van Gogh

Van Gogh was an ardent fan of sunflowers, and I decided to use him as inspiration for this arrangement. To keep it modern, I have plucked all the yellow petals from the sunflowers, which creates a much more interesting, beautiful, and dramatic flower. For this arrangement I picked a turquoise ceramic vase, which works beautifully with the yellows and greens of the sunflowers, but if I had red sunflowers, I would have picked an orange vase. Find a color vase that enhances your flowers for the greatest effect.

8 to 10 *Sunbeam sunflowers (the ones with the yellow centers): cut 3 stems to 20 inches, 4 stems to 18 inches, and 3 stems to 16 inches.*

2 dozen *Sunbright sunflowers (the ones with the dark centers): cut 9 stems to 16 inches and 9 stems to 18 inches; keep 6 stems at 24 inches.*

1 block of oasis

1 tall (approximately 24-inch) vase, preferably in a vivid color

8 to 10 yellow Craspedia

8 to 10 purple echinops

Remove all the yellow petals from the sunflowers the same way you did when you were a teenager: Loves Me, Loves Me Not!

Submerge oasis in water for about 5 minutes.

Put the wet block of oasis in the bottom of your vase, and fill the base with water. The oasis will allow you to stick the sunflowers in any direction you want and will keep them from shifting.

Plant your first Sunbeam sunflower that is about 20 inches long in the middle of the vase. Use the longest stems near the top of the pyramid and the shortest near the bottom.

From there work down in a loose pyramid with the rest of the Sunbeams: after the first flower, add two below it, then add three below the two, then four, and so on.

You will need to leave big gaps between the flowers because you will be going back through the arrangement with each of the other flowers.

Once you have used all the Sunbeams, take eighteen of the Sunbrights cut at 16 and 18 inches, and place them randomly in the gaps between the yellow sunflowers. If you look at the photograph, you will notice that some are facing inward, which is rather beautiful, so don't worry about keeping them all facing out.

Take the remainder of the sunflowers—the six at 24 inches—and place them in the center to add height.

Then last of all, randomly take the Craspedia and echinops pom-poms, and add them in groups of two or three, wherever you see gaps.

sunshine

I find sunflowers to be such happy summer flowers; I love their scale and cheerful round heads. Here I used two varieties, the standard Sunbeams and the more unusual Mahogany sunflowers with yellow and bronze petals. For some extra color I used flowering artichokes. I love the addition of those purple thistles among all that yellow. You can see that this arrangement is much tighter than the other one, and with the glass vase, it feels a little more formal.

1 dozen yellow-centered sunflowers

1 dozen bronze-petaled sunflowers

About 4 flowering artichokes, cut the same height as your vase

About 8 small bronze pom-poms—rudbeckias (echinacea)—cut the same height as your vase

Cut the sunflowers to three different heights.

The first four should be the same height as your vase (mine was about 16 inches), the second group about 18 inches, and the third about 20 inches.

Place the sunflowers in the shortest group around the neck of the vase.

Add the sunflowers in the second group to the vase in the same way, resting them on top of the first group.

Follow those with your last four sunflowers. At this point you should have a dome of sunflowers.

Now, very gently create a gap in the sunflowers (look at the picture; you will see where I have done this, making a space for the purple artichoke flowers and the bronze pom-poms at the front of the arrangement), and place the artichokes and pom-poms in the void.

Be like the flower, turn your faces to the sun.

—KAHLIL GIBRAN

hey, cupcake

While I was in the Container Store looking around, I came across their small reusable "Zig Zag Pots"—they remind me of cupcake holders in wonderful hot colors. If you can't find the exact colors that are in this photograph, bake shops often sell similar containers in metal, which would work just as well. This would be a really cute arrangement for a little girl's birthday party, especially if you intersperse real cupcakes with the flowers.

10 peonies for a large pot

8 peonies for a medium pot

5 peonies for a small pot

Florist's tape or a rubber band

Make little bunches and tie the bouquets together with florist's tape or a rubber band. Then cut the stems very short—a little shorter than the vase so that they rest on the sides. You can apply any large-headed flower to this arrangement—carnations, roses, chrysanthemums, dahlias, and so on.

When a husband brings his wife flowers for no reason, there's a reason.

—MOLLY MCGEE

5 peonies for a small pot

10 peonies for a large pot

8 peonies for a medium pot

upgrade—taking your flowers from coach to business

There is a multitude of combinations you can come up with using pom-poms and other store-bought flowers, such as carnations or chrysanthemums. These arrangements all follow the same principle in terms of how you make the bouquet (see pages 271–273), so once you have grasped that technique, you can have a lot of fun choosing the colors and flowers you want to use.

All of these flowers are arranged in "French bouquets," which are tightly arranged flowers. The flowers are very inexpensive—they can be found almost any-place that sells flowers—but when they are mixed and grouped together by color, they look very chic. Choose flowers in beautiful, vibrant colors with wonderful textures and put them in a pretty and modern vase, which is the key to elevating the bouquet.

pom-pom madness

There is a wide variety of pom-poms out there, but I love these particular ones because of their intense color combined with those purple and yellow centers. These colors remind me of an Yves Saint Laurent collection; he often used these hot colors together. I used two square glass vases to give these country flowers a chic twist. Upgrade any humble deli-bought pom-poms by arranging them in a tight dome and displaying them in colored-glass vases. Everybody looks good in something black, and so do flowers!

3 to 4 dozen purple pom-poms

1 dozen green pom-pom carnations

Florist's wire

You're going to build your bouquet in layers from top to bottom (see pages 271–273), so that you end up holding a round ball of flowers. Tie the stems with florist's wire, and cut them down so that they are the same length as the vase. The blooms should sit on the lip of the vase without showing any stems.

At the end, add in randomly those beautiful green pom-poms.

The same directions apply for the green vase of pink flowers (see page 161).

ROBERT HARRIS   POMPEII

sexpot

I love these magenta chrysanthemums with their divine bleached edges. In the pages 156 and 157, one vase is green wood and the other two are lavender ceramic and black glass. The three different materials give different looks: the black one is very sexy and would be wonderful at night. The lavender arrangement is much cuter and would be pretty outside or in a bedroom, and the green wooden vase, to me, is very Asian—superchic and very fresh. It would be fabulous on an end table in your sitting room.

For the Black Vase

3 dozen Orinoco chrysanthemums

2 dozen amethyst carnations

1 black glass vase (The high shine of the black glass is what makes this arrangement modern and sexy.)

For the Green Vase

2 dozen white football-mum chrysanthemums

1 dozen yellow football-mum chrysanthemums

1 dozen echinops pom-poms

For the Lavender Vase

2 dozen lavender Wish chrysanthemums

1 dozen Matsumoto asters

6 to 8 echinops pom-poms

Florist's wire

You'll need to make these bouquets in your hand and then put them in the vases.

For the black vase, start with the chrysanthemums. Take one flower and then work your way down adding as you go: three, five, seven, and on and on and on. See Bouquet Guide on pages 271–273 to help you.

Try to add as many as you can. Don't worry about the flowers getting squashed.

When you have finished, start adding the carnations, randomly in groups of two or three.

Next, tie the stems with florist's wire.

Cut the stems 2 or 3 inches shorter than the vase so that the arrangement sits on the edge of the vase.

The same principle applies to all three vases.

Fragonard

As I told you before, I often find inspiration in paintings, and this bouquet reminds me of some fabulous eighteenth-century French painters like Fragonard or Boucher. This arrangement is full on! It is big, old school, and fabulous—one that I wanted to do to create a more elaborate look.

Something this formal would be absolutely perfect for a grand entrance or dining room, or a very formal wedding. But it would look most amazing in a totally dilapidated or really simple house because contrast always wins. If it is not high low, then poor and rich work just as well!

1 large block of oasis

2 dozen purple and white (raspberry ripple) English garden roses

1 dozen big thick yellow roses

1 dozen big thick pink roses

½ dozen very deep red roses

6 stems of green leaves (Geranium leaves are very pretty and scented, but you could also use vine or maple leaves.)

6 to 8 stems of mint

3 stems of scabiosa

1 large footed bowl

This is actually fairly easy because the oasis keeps all the stems in place.

Submerge the oasis in water for about 5 minutes. Fit the oasis into the bowl. The fabulous thing about using oasis is how versatile it is: you can play as you go. Use your eye to see that what you are doing is working; if it isn't, you can take the flower out, trim it and stick it in again.

You basically start with the two dozen raspberry ripple roses—place one stem right in the center of the oasis.

Then add the rest of the raspberry ripple roses around that first one.

When you have used all the raspberry ripple roses, start on the yellow ones.

Put the yellow roses in all the holes that you can see, and then keep on going with the rest of the rose varieties until there are none left.

At this point you will have a very handsome arrangement that will impress most people. But it is not enough. You need that extra movement and playfulness to take it a step further.

So this is where you add all the greenery. Just insert the various branches as you please, but make sure that they stick out of the arrangement, creating that movement you are after, as shown in the photograph on the following pages.

6 stems of
green leaves

1 large block of oasis

1 dozen big thick pink roses

3 stems of scabiosa

2 dozen purple and
white (raspberry ripple)
English garden roses

6 to 8 stems
of mint

1 dozen big thick yellow roses

½ dozen
very deep
red roses

bran

cholina

pom-poms

Alliums come in different lengths, but I prefer to keep them very long because I like the height; it adds drama and makes the pom-poms look as though they are floating in the sky.

5 long alliums

4 clear glass bottles (You can really use any bottles, but make sure they are quite heavy to prevent them from tipping over. The ones here are a mixture of laboratory bottles, water bottles, and antique water carafes, which were once used for holding water on a night table. You can find these sorts of things at Bed Bath & Beyond and Wal-Mart, and mix them up with a couple of vintage bottles you find at the flea market. The different shapes are what make the arrangement interesting.)

Start with the longest stem, and cut it just half an inch at the bottom. The tallest allium shown here is about 36 inches.

Then proceed your way down to create the high and low effect: The second one should be 30 inches. The third should be 26 inches. The fourth one should be 22 inches. The last one, 18 inches.

Place the first and the tallest stem in the central bottle, the second in the back right-hand bottle, the third in the central bottle with the tallest, the fourth, in the left-hand bottle, and the last one in the front right-hand bottle.

Placing the bottles on a small stack of books not only gives the arrangement added height but also gives it a stage on which to stand and anchors it on the table.

When you have only two pennies left in the world, buy a loaf of bread with one and a lily with the other.

—CHINESE PROVERB

from Egypt with love

Using the same principle as the "Pom-Poms" recipe, I've created a totally different look. What I like about this arrangement—and it is an easy effect to create—is the tension between the two smaller papyrus stems and the taller one. I love the spikiness of the leaves and the fact that you can see through them, which gives the whole arrangement a lighter, more minimal look.

3 papyrus stems

2 heavy-bottomed vases or bottles

1 cylindrical vase (Make sure the bottle fits at least 10 inches of one stem and has a heavy base so that it doesn't topple over.)

Trim the longest stem to about 36 inches. The stem is very soft on a papyrus so you just have to cut it; don't worry about smashing it.

Cut the second stem to about 20 inches.

Cut the last one to about 10 inches.

Between each stem there should be a big difference in height.

Place the stems in the bottles, reserving the tallest stem for the cylindrical vase.

If we could see the miracle of a single flower clearly, our whole life would change.

—BUDDHA

pleats, please

There is nothing sweet about these round palm leaves—I like their structure and density for a more masculine look. And of course, my favorite part of this arrangement is the pleating of the leaf; it reminds me of Issey Miyake's dresses.

Fan palms are easy to find; they're the most common palms around. You can get them at the flower market, or, if you live in California or Florida, you might even have them in your backyard. Your vases should be about a third to a quarter of the height of your palms, so they won't topple over. You want this arrangement to be more palm than vase; I love how these relatively small bottles are holding these large fan palms. The scale is wonderful.

2 fan palm leaves

2 glass bottles of similar shape and size

These leaves need to overlap for maximum effect. Stand one slightly behind the other, rather than next to it. Cut the taller stem so the total height is about 30 inches. Cut the second stem so the whole palm leaf, from top to bottom, is 24 inches tall.

Afromania

The joy of this arrangement is that it really arranges itself! Lady's mantle's crazy personality means that the more you use, the better it will look. It reminds me of a beautiful Afro, and I LOVE, LOVE, LOVE that spicy, sexy green.

You will need a large vase for this. I have used my trusty trash can, but really any vase with a wide opening will work. When you first buy these bunches, they look very small, but as you shake them out and air gets between the flowers, it really fills out.

8 bunches of Alchemilla mollis (also known as "lady's mantle")

1 large vase or trash can

Take all the stems together and hold them in your hand.

Make sure that they are the same length. You can do this either by standing them up so they all fall to the same length or by simply cutting them so they are even.

When you have them all together in your hand, shake them out so that the bunch starts to fill out. Just like at the hair stylist's when he tips your newly curled head over and teases those tresses.

grass, anyone?

This coffee table arrangement is like a volcanic eruption. There is something very playful about the grasses. It makes me think of a drawing with all the crazy lines falling here and there. You don't have to do anything clever to get this look: trim the stems and stick them in a vase. The grass and gravity will do the rest. If you want to make them shorter, you can cut them, but really the fun is in the height; it reminds me of a Harry Bertoia sculpture.

2 bunches of bear grass

2 glass bottles, one taller than the other

Trim the stems by an inch or two.

Put one bunch in the taller bottle.

Take the remainder of the grass and cut it 3 inches shorter than the first bunch, before putting it in the second vase.

When you let them go, they will take their own course. You can shake them in any direction you want, but really you can leave the grasses to arrange themselves.

wild bunch

For the corner arrangement (page 179), I found this huge bunch of asparagus fern at the flower market, and I was very taken by the scale and delicateness of the leaves. It feels like a cloud to me. Don't be afraid of overscaled foliage. It is very easy to use, and you get a dramatic effect with little effort.

8 stems of asparagus fern (You could also use any tall branch or blossom for this.)

1 huge vase that can hold half to three quarters of the stems.

Trim the stems.

Place in the vase.

Really! That is it. I don't even think it matters if the branches are different heights or not. They will fall and find their own space, which is what gives the arrangement a natural effect.

The world is a rose; smell it and pass it to your friends.

—PERSIAN PROVERB

my all-time favorite decorating tips

Don't put flowers on the floor; it is so "hotel lobby."

Pick a color or a flower that you love and own it and make it your own.

Sometimes things look better in groups, especially along a table. So, start collecting bottles.

I like either one or three of something. I don't like pairs.

Play with scale. I like over-sized anything. Don't be afraid—big flowers, big vases, big furniture all look great in any small environment.

Put something small next to a big arrangement and vice versa; that will give you a good sense of proportion.

If I could, I would have flowers inside my closet! Try to use them in unusual places, or at least in places close to you, even if it is just one rose in a little bottle.

I love mixing fruits and flowers, either in complementing or matching colors.

natural remedy

This photograph speaks for itself. In lieu of flowers, just find a pretty branch in your backyard or a neighbor's and place it in a simple, elegant bottle! You have instant gratification—it looks clean, it brings summer indoors, and it will cost you nothing.

For the vase I used this beautiful old medicine bottle, but any pretty clear bottle will do. Remember to mash the stems with a hammer to allow the branches to drink.

the taller the better

I am only 5 foot 7, so I love tall people and wish I were taller. I am drawn to height, which is why I love using branches. Whether you live in a low-ceilinged apartment or in a palazzo in Beverly Hills, tall arrangements draw your eye up and create a sense of height even if it isn't really there.

I like putting a small arrangement next to a very tall one to intensify the effect. You will find this throughout the book.

For the Branches

10 to 12 tall branches (The Cherry Blossoms shown here are about 8 feet tall.)

1 tall ceramic vase (Ceramic is important because it hides the water, which goes brown very quickly with branches and is hard to change with such a tall arrangement. The weight of the ceramic also helps prevent the tall branches from tipping it over.)

For the Hydrangeas

1 low metal bucket, or you can use any vase

4 to 6 hydrangeas

With a sharp paring knife, split the branches in half, about 4 inches from the bottom. Then, with a hammer, smash the ends a little bit.

Stick them in the vase.

I start with the medium-size, say, 4- or 5-foot-tall ones, and then I keep adding them in order of size, placing the tallest last.

Pair the branch arrangement with the hydrangea bouquet as shown on pages 124–125 (the "Quiet Moment" arrangement).

Flowers are the sweetest things God ever made and forgot to put a soul to.

—HENRY WARD BECKFORD

Olympic Tower

When you have a fabulous view outside your home like this one, you really don't want to (and don't need to) do anything too fussy or complicated. This arrangement costs about $20 but gives you the wow of a $200 bouquet. I love these flowers (they are called "eremurus") because of their extraordinary height and their fabulously modern look. The best thing is that they look great whether you have one, two, or twenty.

1 fabulous glass vase (or a simple glass cylinder) approximately 1½ to 2 feet tall

2 eremurus stems

Cut the stems at different lengths so that the tallest one is four times the height of the vase and the shorter one is three times the height of the vase. You should end up with a nice contrast in height between the two stems.

    Pop them in the vase.

A cynic is a man who, when he smells flowers, looks around for a coffin.

—H. L. MENCKEN

C&C

OMG! Talk about chic and cheap. All you need is a beautiful branch, hopefully from your own backyard, and, failing that, anybody else's! It is a beautiful simple solution because of its height. Always remember: the taller the better. Height adds grandeur to any room.

1 36-inch or taller branch (here I used cherry blossoms)

1 tall vase, at least 24 inches high (The taller and heavier the vase, the taller and heavier the branch can and should be.)

Cut the stem in half and then smash the end with a hammer so that it can drink a lot of water.

Place it in the vase, and fill the vase halfway with water.

When words escape,
flowers speak.

—BRUCE W. CURRIE

so Bill Blass

This would have looked beautiful in Bill Blass's apartment. The beauty of this arrangement is not only the simplicity of using just one type of foliage but also the combination of the deep green leaves with the antique wood center table and the rich brown walls. It is elegant and very handsome. You can achieve this look all year round—this type of foliage has berries perfect for the holiday season. The books really add to the look here.

6 or 8 bunches of green berry viburnum

1 large block of oasis (or three small ones together)

1 large classical-style urn

Florist's wire

This is quite a task, but it is well worth the effort. You need to cut the branches as you build the arrangement, and you have to keep using your eye to make sure the arrangement is full and bushy all the way around. There is no fail-safe method for this.

Before you begin, submerge the oasis in water for about 5 minutes. Place the soaked oasis into the urn.

Start by plunging one of the tallest branches into the oasis from the top, so you have your center.

Then start adding rings all the way around, literally walking in circles as you make it.

The most important thing is to keep walking around the arrangement as you are making it so that it remains even the whole way around.

Keep the branches at different lengths. You need to have some branches that are longer than others so that you have a sense of loftiness among the branches; you don't want a dense bush in the middle of the table!

so weird it's good

I have never been a fan of tropical flowers. HOWEVER, I am crazy about hanging heloconias because not only are they strange looking but they also look like modern sculpture. Hanging heliconias come from the jungle, and you can find them in almost any tropical climate. I see these as objects more than flowers, and I just love how they work with the nineteenth-century medical leg and the stack of rainbow book spines. When you use flowers like this, always consider the surroundings and have fun with it.

1 large colored-glass vase

2 hanging heliconias

Bread feeds the body, indeed, but flowers feed also the soul.

—THE KORAN

make a statement

In this section, you will see the same vase with many different variations of branches, some of which I bought from a flower market and others that I cut from the backyard of my dear friend, Anne McNally. I won't tell you which one is which because the effect is the same. I love any good-looking tall branch. By decorating with branches, you're bringing nature into your home on a dramatic scale—and without having to lug home a heavy houseplant that has roots and dirt.

This series feels like sculpture to me; that is why I had it photographed on pedestals. Believe me, these arrangements will look amazing, and they will change the look of the room the minute they are brought into the house.

I even like these big-statement arrangements in small, low-ceilinged houses, again playing with scale. SO, in my opinion, the taller the BETTER! If you are in the middle of the wilderness, all you have to do is ask your significant other to go for a walk and come back with a beautiful big branch. And a bottle of wine.

Any good-looking tall branch, and I mean any: anything with leaves, blossoms, and especially, during the fall, branches with colorful leaves.

light and airy

I wanted to keep this modern corner in my friend Allison's house very simple. So I found this branch of Kangaroo Paws, which is very light. I love this pale apple green, which I matched to the vase.

3 stems of Kangaroo Paws

1 tall, narrow ceramic vase

This is so simple. Because the branches are so light, they are very easy to arrange, and, because the blossom is so delicate, whichever way the branches stand you'll still achieve a very pretty effect.

I cut the tallest branch to 24 inches and the other two branches to 20 inches.

For scale, add an empty vase next to it. Here I chose a dark and rotund vase—quite the opposite of the tall green ceramic one.

Flowers really do intoxicate me.

—VITA SACKVILLE-WEST

Hawaiian tropic

OMG! Not only is this the easiest arrangement but it is also incredibly cheap! You can find these elephant ears in most gardens and flower markets across the country. Anything oversized is dramatic and always creates a big impact, which is ideal for a party. If you put a small votive candle behind each bottle, the effect of the flame shining through the water will be amazing.

The bottles are all "found"—the biggest one is an old watercooler bottle! And the others are bottles I found at a flea market in Paris. But really, any plain clear bottles you find in any supermarket, like large apple juice bottles, or magnum wine or champagne bottles from the liquor store, would work just as well.

5 bottles in different sizes, very small to very large

5 different tropical leaves (Any large green leaves will do the trick.)

I usually start the tableau with the largest bottle and the largest leaf. That way I have an idea of the space and proportion I have to fill.

From there I start to add the rest of the bottles to the tableau in order of descending size.

Cut the leaves according to the size of the bottle (a few inches of stem should show above the lip of the bottle)—and you have your instant jungle!

when life hands you lemons . . .

This is so simple, it's crazy. If you can't find flowers (or are just tired of them), what better option than to use fruits or vegetables. To me this is the chicest way to dress any table—dining, coffee, or occasional table. You can put this bowl overflowing with lemons ANYWHERE. It reminds me of divine alfresco lunches in Italy.

I bought these Sicilian lemons and limes at the flower market in New York, and they are special because they came with the leaves. But don't panic: any green leaf picked up anywhere will add that same beautiful color.

In the same way that you can use any color combination with flowers, you can also use a variety of fruit combinations with this arrangement. For example, peaches and pears would be beautiful, or green grapes and kiwis, cherry tomatoes and yellow tomatoes, and so on. You're looking for similar shapes but contrasting colors and textures.

About 1 dozen lemons

About 1 dozen limes (depending on the size of your bowl)

Leaves (If the lemons and/or limes come with leaves, great. Otherwise, cut 12 to 14 green leaves that resemble a lemon leaf. Ivy would be very pretty too.)

I like to mix different sizes of bowls, from small to large, all containing a few different types of fruit. For example, a small bowl could contain only small green limes, a medium bowl could have yellow lemons, and the large one a combination of the two.

Once you have placed the fruit in the bowls, add the greenery.

Arrange the leaves between the fruit. You will have to use your eye and see what works with the size of your bowl. In the large bowl, aim for about three clumps of leaves.

1 pine garland the length of your table (You can get this from your florist. Garlands take a lot of time to make and are best left to the professionals.)

Different types of tree trunks (slices and pillars) in white birch, or whatever is available

1 nest, responsibly found (or you can use a fake one)

About 1 dozen white glass balls in different sizes or white ornaments from your own collection

Candles, in interesting colors

1 large bunch of green grapes

1 large white vase

1 tall winter branch (leaves removed)

Narnia

This winter holiday setting reminds me of the scene in *The Chronicles of Narnia* when the little girl opens the door and walks into that beautiful white forest. So people out in the country, go into the forest and find dry branches, white birch trunks, moss, and a nest. Nearly everything here is organic, from the garden or the forest (the completed arrangement is on the next page).

I found the beautiful ceramic trunklike vases at ABC Carpet & Home in New York City, and the birch at the flower market. I use them to give the arrangement height and texture.

I added the fiddlehead ferns for something sculptural, which makes it more modern, and the chartreuse candles and grapes for the color. Be original. Don't use red or cream candles; try orange, hot pink, or purple. Even black would be divine.

To create height and drama, I cut a long branch from the garden for the central vase.

Along the table is an accumulation of different greens. Whatever you can find in your backyard or flower store is good; in this case, I used pine and lemon leaves. For the touches of white, I added two glass balls from ABC Carpet & Home, but you could use any white ornament. Then for the whimsical touch—A (discarded) NEST!

Start by placing your green garland on the table.

If you have a round table, arrange your garland into a circle (like a large nest) in the middle of the table.

Place your large white vase in the middle of the table.

Next, place all your tree trunks down the length of the table, alternating height: short, tall, short, tall.

Add the balls, candles, and fruit randomly among the woods and greens.

Add any other small branches you have into the garland to make it more interesting.

To finish, place the nest at an angle in the center.

hig

h & low

good morning, gorgeous!

Wouldn't you just love to be served breakfast in bed with this coffeepot adorning the tray? We can all dream! In the meantime, this quick and easy arrangement is simply divine next to your bed or on your dressing table. Or if you are feeling very English, set it on the table when you invite your friends over for tea. The elegance of this arrangement comes from mixing high and low—stems, that is. One peony gracefully shades the other. The only major requirements for this "morning glory" are two of the most beautiful peonies you can find. Here they are combined with whimsical polka dots, which makes a charming little scene, but of course you can use any style coffee- or teapot that you have—just try to use one that also has a punchy, whimsical design.

To find the perfect peonies, start by buying four or five, leave them in warm water for a day, and pray to all the gods that two will open this beautifully!

4 to 5 peonies

1 beautiful teapot or coffeepot

Clean the stems by removing all the leaves, except one, near the neck of the longer flower.

Cut the first stem the same height as your teapot or coffeepot so that it will rest on the side of the pot.

Cut the second stem 2 to 3 inches taller than the first. Give the two flowers their own space, but don't allow the stems to show too much.

4 to 5 peonies
(4 of them in pale pink
and 1 of them in hot pink)

1 antique or new teapot
or coffeepot

lots of luck . . .

pretty in pink

This is so pretty I can hardly stand it! When I talk about "high and low," I am not always referring just to size. Have fun mixing heirlooms with inexpensive and brand new pieces. When you start building this arrangement, you'll be grateful to your grandmother that she saved all her old china—and you might even be inspired to start your own flea market collection. I found the pot in the middle in Paris, and the other two are from my favorite store in New York City, Global Table. These *pots de fleurs* are perfect for a luncheon, or if you are feeling very adventurous and DIY, you could collect different pots and use them to decorate a summer wedding. You just need a combination of flea market finds and pieces from stores like Crate&Barrel and Target.

Peonies come in pinks, white, and that fabulous deep red. I suggest using white teapots with pale pink and white peonies, or silver and pewter pots with the deep red and hot pink varieties.

trashy holiday

Who knew that a wastepaper basket from Restoration Hardware could make such a great vase? When you go to places like the Container Store, Pottery Barn, or even Wal-Mart, always take a look at their wastebaskets because you will be amazed at how stylish their shapes and colors are.

This look is perfect for holidays: I love the combination of red, green, and silver (so much chicer than gold). Because of the large scale, I think these "trash can" arrangements are great in an entrance hall or a large dining room.

2 dozen red roses

1 trash can

2 dozen BRIGHT green carnations

The best way to create this arrangement is to make a red rose bouquet (see page 89) and then at the end to randomly add the green splashes of color.

A standard wastebasket is usually about 14 inches high, so the roses should be cut accordingly: the first row along the outside should be about the same height as the can. Then build your bouquet: going around, add an inch or two in height until you've used all the flowers—it is almost like building a small pyramid. Each layer should increase by the size of the rose head (so that you never see stem) on its way to the center.

To make the arrangement slightly three-dimensional (and I do this all the time—it is my signature detail), randomly stuff different flowers into the prepared bouquet. Don't worry if you cover a flower or two when doing this—it's what will give you depth in the bouquet. Once your rose bouquet is complete, place the green carnations within the rose arrangement in random groups or in twos and threes.

trashy gets glam

Can you believe that this beautiful silver container is a trash can? Maybe you can since you saw it in "Trashy Holiday" (page 218), but it is quite amazing how different it looks here. The peonies, chic surroundings, and fabulous purple books elevate this humble trash can to DIVA! Peonies are synonymous with elegance, and they upgrade any arrangement or vessel. I like to have them around all the time. I chose the purple books to pull out the color of the alliums.

2 dozen soft pink peonies

1 silver trash can

5 purple alliums

3 large purple books, jackets removed

Using the bouquet guide on pages 271–273, make a beautiful bouquet with the peonies, until the trash can is completely full.

Then add the alliums in random groups of three or five (as you wish) to the peonies.

Arrange the books in a stack with the largest on the bottom and the smallest on the top; then place the trash can on top of the books.

Can we conceive what humanity would be if it did not know the flowers?

—MAURICE MAETERLINCK

yellow submarine

When I am styling for a magazine photo shoot, I always look around and try to find a color in the room that catches my eye, whether it is on a pillow, the carpet, or the furniture. In this case, the fabulous yellow chair inspired me to use these three beautiful yellow peonies. I created the high/low effect I like so much by using the two tiers of the table, as well as a tall and a short vase.

3 yellow peonies

2 bud vases of different heights

Cut the stems different heights for each vase. For the taller vase, cut one stem the length of the vase and other stem a couple of inches shorter. For the smaller vase, cut the stem a little shorter than the vase so that the bloom just rests on the lip of the vase.

A rose is a rose is a rose is a rose.

—GERTRUDE STEIN

oh, Andy!

I just LOVE mixing really inexpensive and expensive things. As you can see in the picture, almost everything is expensive: all that silver and the second-century Ming object are priceless. But the hula girl and the flowers are as cheap as they come. I love these pom-poms, otherwise known as "gomphrena." You can find them just about anywhere; I got these at a deli near my apartment.

3 bunches of hot pink gomphrena

3 bunches of orange gomphrena

1 stout ceramic vase with a wide neck (Here, the rustic pot contrasts with the glamorous surroundings [a silver vase would be great too], and if you placed it on a long table, it would look rich and extravagant.)

Cut the flower stems so that they are an inch or so taller than the neck of the vase.

I like to fill half the vase with pink pom-poms and the other half with orange for a color-blocked look.

Robert John Thornton   The Temple of Flora   TASCHEN

paradise on
24th street

Orchids are one of my top-three favorite flowers, along with peonies and English garden roses.

I love them because they come in different sizes, shapes, and colors and they last a long time whether they are in water or planted. You can find them in almost any supermarket and certainly at any nursery across the country.

This picture, taken in my living room, is an EXPLOSION of color! I collect little bottles and vases, which are so useful when you want to achieve a tableau like this. The inspiration for this comes from the altars that you see in South East Asia, where many of these orchids originate.

You can achieve this look with any flower; the key is to mix as many colors and varieties as possible.

A variety of hybrid phalaenopsis orchids

Gather together small vases and bottles, and depending on what you have, use them accordingly: a little vase will hold one orchid; a medium vase will hold two.

Remember to apply the high/low concept: one high, one short; one high, one short.

It is easiest when you start with the tallest orchids, placing them in the center of the table and randomly working down in size and around the whole table. It helps to add two or three interesting objects from around your house to mix up the display.

purple rain

Purple and lavender are my favorite colors in the WHOLE world, but what really make this arrangement are the planted orchids. Planted orchids are elegant and economical: they last about six weeks and sometimes even longer if they are well looked after (all they need is good light and a little water once a week). Orchids are like sculptures—they are beautiful objects but with flowers. And they are a great block for an undesirable corner or view! I love the symmetry of using two—of course, one taller than the other. If both plants are the same height, you can create the high/low effect by putting one on a small stack of books.

To intensify the color, I used a cut version of the same orchid in front of the daybed. This makes a stunning impression when you walk in the room, especially if you choose an orchid that coordinates with something in the room, as I have done here with the pillows.

scary movie

The combination of black and white is a great foil for color. You can see how the chartreuse and yellow just pop in front of this fabulous graffiti painting. This is simple to do. Find two different-colored cymbidiums—the yellow and green are great together, but they come in many colors, so have fun choosing your combination.

3 cymbidiums

1 tall colored-glass bottle vase

2 small oval ceramic vases (in two sizes)

Trim the stems on two of the cymbidiums, leaving them the same length as each other.

Place them in the tall glass bottle, and let their own weight take them in the direction they want to go.

Take the third stem and cut the top off. This will give you the orchid for the smallest vase.

Cut the remainder of the third stem so that it is an inch shorter than the medium vase and pop it in.

Flowers are restful to look at. They have neither emotions nor conflicts.

—SIGMUND FREUD

heaven on earth

I found these antique bottles at what I think is the most divine shop in New York City: De Vera. It really is heaven on earth. You will find beautiful things there from all over the world. These particular bottles are from Venice, Italy.

Italy is well known for its blown glass, and even though it is very fragile and precious, one really shouldn't be afraid of using it. Beautiful things are meant to be used, not just admired.

And as you can see, this composition of simple stems, foils for the vases, works beautifully on a mantelpiece. It would be lovely by your bed, too, or in any corner. And of course, it would be divine in the middle of your dining table with a crisp linen cloth and that butterfly hovering on the lychee. For this setup I used a taxidermy butterfly from Evolution in Manhattan, but you can get paper ones on garlands, which would work just as well. Add some humor or slightly unexpected objects to your arrangement, especially when you are using your precious pieces: humor prevents the whole arrangement from feeling too uptight.

1 beautiful bottle

1 beautiful carafe

1 beautiful footed bowl
    (A small glass cake stand
    or delicate glass bowl would
    also work.)

What's most important is that the shapes of the vessels are different. You see how the silhouette of the carafe is quite different from that of the spiral bottle, and the bowl adds a different height.

Here I am basically copying a Dutch Old Master's still life. They always had fruit in their paintings, and you can use any small, seasonal fruit that you like, such as strawberries, kumquats, or plums.

beautiful dirt

5 bottles (Odd numbers make a
   better composition than even
   numbers.)

1 green alabaster or marble
   bowl (It could be any color—
   just make sure your fruit
   matches!)

8 green figs

6 to 8 English garden roses
   (The beauty of an English
   garden rose is the fine stem.
   That is actually what I LOVE
   about them, and it gives the
   flower some agility.)

I ADORE the dirt on these old medicine bottles that I found at a flea market in Paris. It is the dirt that gives them that beautiful patina, and, of course, they are my favorite color, lavender!

This is the perfect example of how a simple old bottle covered in dirt can be used to create a beautiful moment like this.

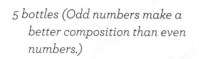

the odd couple

This arrangement is like an opposites-attract couple. Tall people often like short people, flamboyant people go for quiet people, and so on. This arrangement is a perfect example of mixing scale and how well it can work. I love doing this type of high/low arrangement, and so I do, all the time. The cool thing about this look is the vases: I wrapped each ordinary glass cylinder with some fabulous paper, which turned the vase into something quite special. The possibilities with this idea are endless because you can use any kind of art paper, wallpaper, or fabric.

1 24-inch cylindrical vase

1 12-inch cylindrical vase

2 sheets of an interesting paper, such as wallpaper, wrapping paper, or Japanese art paper

Double-sided tape

15 hydrangea stems (These can be either short- or long-stemmed; it doesn't matter.)

18 hot pink carnations

18 purple carnations

For the Vases: Cut the paper to the same length as your vase.

Put a strip of double-sided tape on one edge of the paper, and stick the paper to the vase.

Curl the paper around the vase, securing the other end of the paper where the two edges meet with tape.

Repeat this for the second vase.

For the Hydrangea Bouquet: If you have the long-stemmed variety, then cut the stems so that they are slightly shorter than your vase.

Start your bouquet with the first ring of about five hydrangeas resting on the side of the vase.

Next, place five more flowers in a second layer on top of the first.

Then add the last five, at random, to the arrangement to add depth.

For the Carnation Bouquet: Cut the stems so that they are slightly shorter than the vase.

Just as you did with the hydrangea bouquet, place a first layer of about eight pink carnations around the edge of the smaller vase.

Next, place the rest of the pink carnations in a second layer on top of the first.

Then, add the purple ones randomly throughout the bouquet.

little and large

Pairing tall flowers and foliage with flowers cut short is one of my signature styles. I always do this at home or on my photo shoots. Like your big brother walking with your little sister, I like to put something really tall and big beside something simpler and smaller. Sometimes, as shown here, I keep the flowers to a similar palette, but sometimes, for a more casual look, I like to use more random colors, like deep purple cherry blossoms and yellow-orange carnations. This contrast in scale will wake up an entrance hall or any dead corner of your house.

*About ½ bale of lilacs
    (approx. 30 stems)*

1 tall ceramic vase

2 to 3 fully open peonies

1 glass of water

Lilacs: Clean the lilacs by removing all the green leaves.
    Smash the ends of the stems with a hammer.
    Place them in the vase, starting with the shorter stems around the edge of the vase (they should be the same length as the vase).
    Then build your bouquet inward. With each inner ring of lilacs, add about 3 inches to the stems.
    When this arrangement is finished, you can add two or three tall stems to the middle of the bouquet, which will create more height.

Peonies: Cut the peonies at two different heights, and put them in the glass of water.
    Place the peonies next to the vase of lilacs.

the best reasons to bring flowers

For no reason is really the best, best.

After a great, sexy night.

After you lie!

For good news.

Send flowers to yourself! I send flowers to myself all the time. Don't wait for anyone to send you flowers.

To be polite (or to suck up).

Because you can't cook.

To celebrate anything.

Because they're expected ...
sooner or later.

Because you now know that a fabulous
arrangement won't break the bank!

half and half

I LOVE dividing a vase in half with flowers. This is just another way of doing flowers, but what I really love here is the combination of scale. I used magical emerald hydrangeas, which have very small and delicate petals that are fabulous when mixed with the much bigger, fatter, fuller rose.

5 stems of magical emerald hydrangeas

1 dozen peony roses

1 dark ceramic vase

Cut the stems of both the hydrangeas and the roses about 2 inches shorter than your vase, so that the blooms will rest on the vase's lip.

Start with the hydrangeas by putting the first three stems in the vase, resting them on one side of it.

Then add the next two by resting them on top of the first three.

Now place your roses around the edge of the vase, resting them on the side opposite the hydrangeas.

Then add them on top of each other until you have a beautiful dome bouquet of roses leaning against the hydrangeas.

To create a little flower is the labor of ages.

—WILLIAM BLAKE

orchid mania

For this dining room table, I used a grouping of various chartreuse and black glass bottles with a colorful mix of cattleya orchids. I think the effect is both vibrant and modern. Very often your flower arrangement is as dependent on your collection of vases and bottles as it is on the flowers you are using. So keep collecting! This type of setting could be achieved with any bottles and any flowers.

6 medium bottles

6 small bottles (Use bottles in two contrasting colors, if possible.)

12 cattleya orchids in a variety of colors

Place the bottles on the table so that you get a zigzag of colors and heights.

Cut your orchids a little shorter than the vases.

let's dance

In this arrangement the flowers look like dancing partners; their long stems and bobbing heads give a sense that they are about to start moving to the music! The key here is mixing long- and short-stemmed flowers. Have fun when you are arranging, and give your flowers some personality.

Gerberas look like the flowers that children draw, and they come in bright and cheerful colors. They are so ordinary that you can find them almost anywhere all year long. This is a great arrangement for a kid's birthday. Have fun finding your color combination. A multicolored group would look fabulous, but don't go overboard—never more than three colors.

These "vases" are all recycled bottles from my kitchen—olive oil, tomato salsa, lemonade, and various condiment jars. It doesn't matter what type of bottle or jar you use; what is important is that they are all different sizes and heights. What could be cheaper and more eco-friendly?

12 to 16 gerberas in two or three colors

Several mismatched bottles and kitchen jars

Ultimately you want a tall and zigzagging arrangment, so leave the stems predominantly long, just trimming them to different lengths. Place the tall ones in the higher-necked bottles and shorter ones in the little jars. Arrange them as you go: short, tall, short, tall.

The great thing about using bottles for these flowers is that the tight neck will hold the tall stems in place.

Once you have filled all the bottles, you can either place the arrangement directly on the table, or, to give them more height, you can put them on an upturned tray—a stage (on which to dance!).

*mismatching bottles
and kitchen jars*

TOMATE
PRÉPARATION À BASE
DE VINAIGRE ET DE
PULPE DE TOMATE
A L'OLIVIER PRODUIT 200ml
À PARTIR DE FRUITS FRAIS

FRUIT PASSION
LA PASSION
PRÉPARATION À BA
DE VINAIGRE ET DE
DE FRUIT DE LA PA
A L'OLIVIER PRODUIT

12 to 16 gerberas

sweet & low

Even though the effect is gorgeous, the principles of this arrangement are very simple. In fact, the colors of the ceramic cake stand and the vases work together to create most of the impact: the white of the stand becomes a foil for the turquoise of the vases. The variety of shapes, sizes, and textures is key. The vases here are very small; the tallest is only 6 inches, but to add DRAMA and to give them the height of a centerpiece, I've used a cake stand. Cut the flower stems so that they stand an inch or two above the top of the bud vases. Display the vases on the cake stand by height.

*5 to 7 English garden roses
(You could also use
ranunculuses or anemones.)*

1 cake stand

*3 little bud vases
(in different heights
and shapes)*

Christmas in the tub

Don't be boring! Do Christmas in the bathroom. Of course, it helps if you have a bathroom the size of this one, but any bathroom can take a pine garland. Imagine the smell in the morning.

I don't like Christmas decorations much; in fact, I NEVER use them. When I do Christmas in my house, it is usually all green foliage. Here, I used two different green garlands (see pages 254–255). They almost look as though they have been flung at the window because they are not perfectly centered. To add that red Christmassy touch, I made various arrangements in deep reds, purples, and hot pink carnations. They are super-inexpensive and look very festive when grouped together.

Garlands

1 15-foot garland and 1 25-foot garland, both 8 to 10 inches thick, depending on the size of your window and your preference

For the Carnation Arrangements

2 dozen red carnations

2 dozen purple carnations

2 dozen hot pink carnations

Florist's wire

Florist's tape

For the Garlands: Because garlands are very difficult to make, save yourself three days' hard work by calling your florist and ordering a beautiful garland. Time is money, and the money you spend on buying this garland will be well worth the time you save for yourself.

Ask for a mixture of fir, pine, lemon leaf, and magnolia. If you manage to get those four together, it's perfect. If you want to get more elaborate, you can add branches with blackberries.

Any florist in the country can make a beautiful green garland for you, and most will charge by the foot.

Garlands are quite simple to drape on the window.

Put a nail at each end of the window frame.

Leave 4 to 5 feet of your garland hanging on the left side of the window.

Hook the garland around the nail with a piece of florist's wire.

Then swag the garland as deep as you like in front of the window.

Pin it on the right-hand side in the same way you did on the left.

Leave the remainder to hang down the side.

Start with 6 to 8 feet of the second garland from the right-hand side.

Go up as before, hooking the garland, and then swag the center, making sure that this garland hangs either higher or lower than the first one.

Then pin it as before on the other side, and let the remainder hang down.

For the Carnation Arrangements: Cut all of the carnations very short. (They don't need to hold themselves up in the vase because they are going to rest on the top. They just have to reach the water.)

Start with one carnation, then take two or three more (depending on the size of the vase) and wrap them around the first. Carry on in this manner until you have a bunch that is big enough to rest on top of your vase. Tie with florist's tape.

Arrange the vases by color for a stronger effect. I've also found that bouquets arranged by color are more vibrant than bouquets with assorted colors, which is why, in this instance, I have not added my signature random flowers. The only important detail here is that the three vases need to be different heights to create the high and low contrast that I love. I used antique vases, but you can really use any vases that you have on hand.

To add a touch of drama, add a few candles, but please don't burn the house down!

Christmas without ornaments

I collect bottles throughout the year, and you can do that so easily too: at flea markets around the country you will find beautiful bottles in abundance. So start buying them by color groups. TRUST ME, when the specific time comes, like Christmas, you will call to thank me!

Instead of using boring and traditional ornaments and balls on top of your mantel and coffee table, simply group green and red bottles together OR just green bottles together OR just red bottles together.

The more the merrier. In this case I grouped red and green bottles—they are all different heights, which creates a visually interesting effect, even though the bottles are just flea market finds.

TA-DAAA!

4 red amaryllis stems

6 bottles in Christmassy colors (or as many as you want)

5 lovely ferns from your backyard or local park (Really, any green foliage will do.)

1 green candle

1 candlestick

Cut the stems so that the amaryllis blooms sit in various heights in the bottles (some very high, some very close to the lip of the bottle). Arrange the blooms and the foliage in the bottles. The trick here is not to feel that every bottle needs a flower. Here, I've left two bottles empty, but the abundance of bottles still makes the arrangement feel complete. Set the candle where you think it looks best, and grab the matches.

the color purple

The real beauty of this arrangement is found in the contrasts of the colors, the shapes, and the textures, which keep the arrangement whimsical while allowing me to use what I have on hand—no special shopping necessary. I love how the colors here not only bounce off one another but complement one another as well. The softness of the sweet pea against the more rigid texture of the anemones and the peony also pleases me enormously. As for colors, my favorite deep hues are purples and reds. Here, I have put together a combination of those colors in different vases that have the anticipated large-medium-small scale.

What is even more different and surprising here—and I LOVE doing this from time to time—is that the arrangements mimic the pattern and material in the tablecloth. Not only do the blooms echo the embroidered flowers but the pewter and glass reflect the silvery silk dupioni, all of which work together to unify the elements on the table.

About 4 dozen sweet peas

1 tall vase

1 dozen blue anemones

1 medium vase

1 fully open peony in dark red

1 small vase (just large enough to fit 1 peony)

1 floral tablecloth in a similar palette as your flowers

Florist's tape

Sweet Peas: Grab all four dozen sweet peas, and cut the stems evenly so they are all the same length.

Then jam them in the tall vase and tease (gently) like a crazy hairdo.

Anemones: The same principle applies as did to the sweet peas. Tie them together with a little florist's tape, and cut them very short, so that they sit in the vase.

Pop them in the medium vase.

Peony: Cut it to the size of the vase so the bloom will rest on the side of the vase lip.

Put it in the small vase.

jungle fever

In my friend Santiago's dining room, he has the most amazing photograph from the *Jungle Series* by Thomas Struth. The photograph is very dense and dark; so to brighten the table, I added two different colors of orchids, my FAVORITE flower. Interestingly, rather than clashing with the orchids, the dark backdrop became a wonderful foil for their intense colors. What's even more exciting in this mix is not just the colors of the orchids and how they complement each other (though very *fashionable,* darling) but the rigid cymbidium orchids, which pretty much always stand up, alongside the soft and droopier phalaenopsis orchids.

2 stems of cymbidium orchids (the green ones)

3 glass vases, in different shapes but similar heights (Vases with bottle necks work well as they hold the stems upright.)

2 stems of pink phalaenopsis orchids (the droopy ones)

Cut the cymbidium stems by about 2 inches, keeping them quite tall and at different heights, approximately 18 and 14 inches long. Place them in two of your vases.

Take the phalaenopsis stems and cut them to different lengths and shorter than the cymbidium stems. Pop them in the remaining vase.

Flowers are beautiful hieroglyphics of nature, with which she indicates how much she loves us.
—WOLFGANG VON GOETHE

three graces

You don't need to spend a lot of money to add a splash of glamour or color to an unassuming corner in your home. As you can see here, all I did was find three beautiful peonies in a deep pink to pull out the red of the lampshade and the chair. And to make it more fun, I used a pretty green Japanese vase.

3 long-stemmed peonies

1 vase

Trim at an angle the stem of the tallest peony by about half an inch.

Cut the second peony (also at an angle) about 6 inches shorter than the first.

Cut the last stem just a couple of inches shorter than the second, creating a visual relationship between the two and leaving the first one to rise alone.

I'd rather have roses on my table than diamonds on my neck.

—EMMA GOLDMAN

unexpected combination

Some people might think that these delphiniums would look prettier in a white or blue vase; I think they look more interesting with this coral ceramic bottle. This is the perfect way to spice up a monochromatic room—the pillows also help a lot! But it is amazing how three or four simple stems standing tall and bright can breathe life into a room.

4 blue delphiniums

1 lily

1 coral-glazed ceramic vase

1 green vase

1 empty perfume bottle

For the Coral Vase: Cut three delphinium stems so that the overall height is about 4 feet tall.

For the Green Vase: Cut the remaining delphinium stem so that it is about 2½ feet tall.

For the Lily: Cut the lily stem very short so that the flower just pokes out the top of the perfume bottle.

Let us be grateful to people who make us happy; they are the charming gardeners who make our soul blossom.

—MARCEL PROUST

zesty morning

I really believe that you HAVE TO HAVE flowers in your bathroom. There is nothing more appealing than being met by fresh flowers first thing in the morning. Here, the inspiration came from the beautiful lemons in the still life painting propped up on the basin. I chose yellow lilies with these green Japanese vases because I love their curvy shapes—and isn't it interesting how the shapes of the vases mimic those of the lemons in the painting?

3 yellow Asiatic lilies

3 green ceramic vases in different heights

Keeping it very tall, cut the first lily stem and put it in the tallest vase.

Cut the second lily stem about 4 inches shorter than the first.

Cut the third so that only 2 inches of stem peek out from the top of the vase.

Flowers are love's truest language.

—PARK BENJAMIN

red is the color

I was inspired by the red bindings of all the Sotheby's catalogs in this room: I love how they have been grouped by color, which is why I chose three red peonies. But any red flower would have worked, or indeed any color, because you will want to match whatever color grouping is going on in your room. (I like to find a color in a room to match the flower to, which I always do in photo shoots.) To add another punch of color, so that the red doesn't disappear, I chose these apple green Japanese vases to throw things off a little—not everything needs to be matchy-matchy!

3 perfect red peonies, or any red flowers such as roses or carnations (The choice of flowers depends on what you are matching: a sunflower could have worked here as well to pull out the yellow in the artwork.)

2 small ceramic vases

Remove all the leaves, and cut the stems of your peonies.
   Take the first one and cut it so that it is about an inch taller than the vase you are using.
   Keep the two remaining flowers long.
   Cut one to about 12 inches high and the other to about 18 inches high.

Just living is not enough . . . One must have sunshine, freedom, and a little flower.

—HANS CHRISTIAN ANDERSEN

bouquet guide

Here is a simple guide to making my trademark bouquet, which you can apply to pretty much any flowers.

1. Holding one flower stem, add two more stems so that you make a pyramid shape, with one stem slightly higher than the other two. The tops of the two flowers should touch the base of the first bloom (you don't want to see any stem).

1.

2. 3.

4. 5.

2. Add three more stems around the base of the two blooms, again, being careful not to show any stem. Then add another five or six below the three in the same fashion.

3. Secure them with florist's tape or a rubber band.

4. Clip the stems about two inches shorter than the vase so that the bouquet sits on the bottom of the vase (flowers should cover the edge of the vase).

5. Finally, randomly add in groups of two or three flowers to the bouquet. This makes it more three-dimensional and gives it that crazy look, which I LOVE.

That is IT!

places around the house that are just perfect for flowers

On pedestals in entrance halls— when you walk into your house the first thing you see should be a flower.

To divide a room: place large branches in vases and set them on a skinny table or chairs between the two spaces.

When you have a party, fill the bathrub with paperwhites. (They're expensive, but divine!)

In the bathroom—think of how nice it would be to see a rose instead of your sleepy morning face!

In the kitchen, use something with more volume, like ferns or carnations.

On window sills: they are so often ugly—especially in NYC apartments. Just a few bottles with a couple of stems and the light coming through the glass are so pretty.

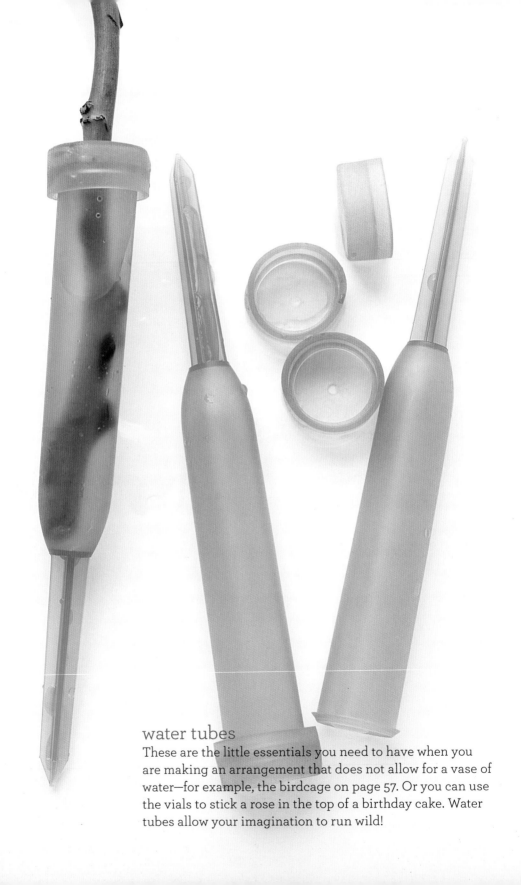

water tubes

These are the little essentials you need to have when you are making an arrangement that does not allow for a vase of water—for example, the birdcage on page 57. Or you can use the vials to stick a rose in the top of a birthday cake. Water tubes allow your imagination to run wild!

overscaled scissors

I think that I like these as much because they are chic as because they are really better than normal-sized scissors. But they are very good for cutting paper or any soft-stemmed flowers, and when you have pretty scissors, you are more likely to take the time to cut the stems on your flowers and be inspired to make something beautiful.

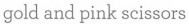

gold and pink scissors
These are good for any flowers with soft stems such as pom-poms, carnations, or peonies.

clippers
Essential for any flowers with hard stems such as hydrangeas, branches, or roses.

wire and florist's tape
These two are great for holding tight bouquets in place. You will see that I refer to one or the other in almost every arrangement in this book.

Swiss Army knife

This is my favorite tool of all. It is so small and easy to store, and it is strong enough to cut anything from branches to tulips.

oasis

Oasis blocks are great when you are building a bouquet in a shallow vase or when you have to cut flowers short and you don't want them to flop around. A slab of oasis can be cut and shaped to fit your vessel. Soak it prior to placing it in the vase so your flowers can drink while standing at attention.

FISHS EDDY

We do dishes.

DE VERA

THE END OF HISTORY
548 1/2 HUDSON ST. NYC. 10014
TEL. 212.647.7598

WWW.GLOBALTABLE.COM
GLOBAL TABLE
107-109 SULLIVAN ST. NYC 10012
T 212.431.5839   F 212.431.5892

966-

JMCF.

MADELINE
WEINRIB

TREIL

418 East
New York, N
Tel. (212
Fax. (212

Howard Christian

DAVID MORSA
DIRECTOR

RESTORATION HARDWARE

RO

ARLANE

STREET
NY 10013
12 966 2996 FA

OSTUDIOS COM
OS COM

PAPER PRESENTATION.COM
23 WEST 18 STREET, NYC 10011
T: 212.463.7035   F: 212.463.7022
INFO@PAPERPRESENTATION.COM

G E

1

@treillageny.com

Pearl River
珠江百貨公司

always something new at the store

477 Broadway, New York, NY 10013 Tel: (212)431-4770
Shopping online: www.pearlriver.com Mail order: 1-800-878-2446

resources

resources

design services and retailers

Any flea market in the world, especially in Paris and the Portobello Road Market in London.

ABC Carpet & Home, Inc.
888 Broadway
New York, NY 10003
212-473-3000
www.abchome.com

Aero
Julia McFarlane
419 Broome Street
New York, NY 10013
212-966-1500
www.aerostudios.com

Anthropologie
www.anthropologie.com for store locations and online ordering

Bed Bath & Beyond
www.bedbathandbeyond.com for store locations and online ordering

Clio
92 Thompson Street
New York, NY 10012
212-966-8991
www.clio-home.com

The Container Store
www.containerstore.com for store locations and online ordering

Crate&Barrel
www.crateandbarrel.com for locations and online ordering

De Vera
Two locations:
1 Crosby Street
New York, NY 10013
212-625-0838

29 Maiden Lane
San Francisco, CA 94108
415-788-0828

The End of History
548½ Hudson Street
New York, NY 10014
http://theendofhistoryshop.blogspot.com

Evolution
120 Spring Street
New York, NY 10012
212-343-1114
evolnyc@aol.com

Fisher & Page
150 West 28th Street
New York, NY 10001
212-255-3196

Fishs Eddy
889 Broadway
New York, NY 10003
212-420-9020
www.fishseddy.com

Pierre Frey Fabrics
www.pierrefrey.com for locations

Global Table
109 Sullivan Street
New York, NY 10012
212-431-5839
www.globaltable.com

Gracious Home
www.gracioushome.com for store locations and online ordering

Margaret Neiman Harber
Kaleidakolor Calligraphy Studio
201 East 17th Street, 5C
New York, NY 10003
212-475-1653
www.kkolorink.com

Housing Works Thrift Shops
www.housingworks.org for store locations
www.shophousingworks.com for online ordering

Calvin Klein Home Collection
www.calvinklein.com for online ordering

Liz O'Brien
800A Fifth Avenue
New York, NY 10065
212-755-3800

Ochre
462 Broome Street
New York, NY 10013
212-414-4332
www.ochre.net
www.ochrestore.com

Paper Presentation.com
28 West 18th Street
New York, NY 10011
1-800-PAPER-01 (727-3701)
www.paperpresentation.com

Pearl River
477 Broadway
New York, NY 10013
212-431-4770
www.pearlriver.com

Pottery Barn
www.potterybarn.com for store locations and online ordering

Restoration Hardware
www.restorationhardware.com
for locations and online ordering

John Rosselli Antiques
306 East 61st Street
Ground Floor
New York, NY 10065
212-750-0060
www.johnrosselliantiques.com

Takashimaya New York
693 Fifth Avenue
New York, NY 10022
1-800-753-2038; 1-212-350-0100
www.takashimaya-ny.com

Wal-Mart
www.walmart.com for store
locations and online ordering

West Elm
www.westelm.com for store
locations and online ordering

Williams Sonoma
www.williams-sonoma.com
for store locations and online
ordering

Madeline Weinrib Atelier
ABC Carpet & Home
(available through various retail-
ers)
888 Broadway, 6th floor
New York, NY 10003
212-473-3000, ext. 780
www.madelineweinrib.com

flower wholesalers and garden supplies

Caribbean Cuts
120 West 28 Street
New York, NY 10001
212-924-6969
www.caribbeancuts.com

Dutch Flower Line, Inc.
148 West 28th Street
New York, NY 10001
212-727-8600

Foliage Garden
120 West 28th Street
New York, NY 10001-6109
212-989-3089
www.foliagegarden.com

Home Depot
www.homedepot.com for store
locations and online ordering

Jamali Garden Supplies
149 West 28th Street
New York, NY 10001
212-244-4025
www.jamaligarden.com

Gary W. Page
120 West 28th Street
New York, NY 10001
212-741-8928

Planter Resource
150 West 28th Street
New York, NY 10001
212-206-POTS (7687)
www.planterresource.com

Treillage, Ltd.
418 East 75th Street
New York, NY 10021
212-535-2288
www.treillageonline.com

U.S. Evergreen
805 Sixth Avenue
New York, NY 10001
212-741-5300

Whole Foods Market
www.wholefoodsmarket.com for
store locations

GRACIAS!

The time between the idea for this book and its completion was very short! It is therefore the focus, enthusiasm, and hard work of a few special friends and colleagues that have made it possible for me to take my original idea and turn it into a book.

To my dear friends Allison Sarofim, Anne McNally, Santiago Gonzalez, and Adam Lippes, I would like to thank you for allowing me to shoot in your wonderful houses.

My immense gratitude to Lucio Romero for so generously lending your eye on shoots, and your time and amazing energy throughout.

I would like to thank from the bottom of my wallet Isabel Parra, William Waldron's divine assistant, for generously giving so many extra days to the shoot.

To my driver, Kazi, you are a sweetheart to me! Thank you for your patience while I was a screaming passenger on our crazy car rides around New York in the pouring rain.

I would like to thank Margaret Russell, the talented editor in chief at *Elle Decor*. It is thanks to the magazine that I have been exposed to so many chic rooms and have been able to style them with such beautiful flowers over the last eight years.

At the flower market, Gary Page, Chris De Meo, and Casper Trat, thank you for your invaluable help during the process of selecting and buying flowers for this book.

Natalie at Global Table, I love your store, and thank you for being such a support and inspiration to me over the years.

To William Waldron and English rose Rita Konig, thank you for keeping up with my concord pace and making it such fun along the way.

AND thank you, Doris Cooper, my editor at Clarkson Potter, for clipping my pages in *Elle Decor* and having the *cojones* to suggest a flower book in such an uncertain financial climate. To Angelin Borsics, Doris's lovely assistant, for her hard work, and Marysarah Quinn for designing such a beautiful book—and finally to the real stars: the flowers!

gracias

Carlos

index

Alchemilla mollis, 175, 177
alliums, 170–71
altar arrangement, 226–27
amaryllis, 257
anemones, 94–95, 258–59
antiques, 217, 232–35
artichokes, 96–97
    flowering, 149
artworks, as inspiration,
    58–63, 126–27, 164–67,
    231, 261, 266
asparagus fern, 179, 181
autumn colors, 80–81
azalea, 54–55

baby's breath, 67
baby shower, 42
baby slippers, 42–43
bacteria prevention, 13
bags
    colorful plastic, 38–39
    shopping, 90–91
bamboo steamer, 76–79
bathroom
    Christmas decoration,
        252–55
    flowers in, 266–67, 274–75
bento box, 48–49
birdcage, 56–57
bird's nest, 208, 210–11
black glass vessels, 160, 162,
    163, 244–45
books, as elevation, 53,
    98–105, 126–27, 160,
    170–71, 178, 180, 220–21
bottles
    in Christmas colors, 257
    green glass, 82–89
    grouping of, 26–27, 182,
        232–35, 244–49, 256–57
    laboratory, 28–29, 170, 171
    orange and yellow, 80–81
    perfume, 264–65
    Perrier and beer, 82–89
    salsa, 16–17
    varying sizes, 204–5,
        246–49
    vintage, 170–71, 232–35
bouquet guide
    assembly steps, 271–73
    bundling, 89, 106
    clumping, 120–21
    dome shape, 89, 158–61,
        242–43
    rose bouquet, 88–89, 93,
        164–67, 218
    tight packing, 65, 122–23
    See also French bouquet
bowls, 18–21, 50–51
    footed, 164, 166–67,
        232–35
boxes, 35, 36

bento, 48–49
    from fruit, 44–45
    as pedestal, 110–11
branches, 184–91, 198–203,
    208–9
    as room divider, 274

cacti, 19–21
cake stands, 54–55, 232,
    250–51
candles, 208, 210–11, 257
cans
    with colorful labels, 17
    from paint, 92–93
carafes, 170, 171, 232, 233
carnations, 155, 156–61, 163,
    236–37, 275
    in book arrangement,
        98–99
    in Christmas bathroom
        arrangement, 252, 253,
        254–55
    in NY logo coffee mug, 27
    in plastic take-out con-
        tainers, 122–23
    in rose bouquet, 218–19
cattleya orchids, 244–45
centerpieces
    bamboo steamer, 76–79
    bento boxes, 48–49
    birdcage with vine, 56–57
    paint can, 92–93
    soup tureen, 94–95
    in tablecloth motif, 258–59
    yellow and orange bottles,
        80–81
ceramic vases
    Japanese green, 262–63,
        266–67
    rustic/wide neck, 224–25
    for silk flowers, 136–37
    strong colors, 61, 72–75,
        89, 109, 110–11, 124–25,
        130–33, 138–39, 143,
        146–47, 202–3, 250–51,
        264–65
    for tall branches, 186–87,
        190–91, 198–203
    white, 208, 210–11
chartreuse, 136–37
    bottles, 244–45
    roses, 108–11, 130–31
    watering can, 112–15
chili peppers, 116–19
Christmas decorations,
    252–57
chrysanthemums, 154–57,
    160–63
    Chinese arrangement,
        128–29
    lavender and purple,
        126–27
    See also pom-poms
coffee cups, 30–33
    New York logo, 24–27

coffee mugs, graphic, 68–69
coffeepots, 214–17
color, 138–49, 158–61, 163,
    182, 246
    as accent, 262–65
    artwork-inspired, 58–59,
        260–61
    black/white foil for, 230–31
    consistency in, 138–39
    grouping by, 99, 136, 155,
        268–69
    guide for using, 142–43
    hot, 130–31, 139, 155,
        158–61
    mixing and matching,
        88–89, 93, 142
    monochromatic, 99
    seasonal choices, 80–81,
        99, 143
    vases arranged by, 254
cupcake holders, 150–53
cups, 30–33
currents, 48–49
cylinders, 172–73, 174, 189
    paper-wrapped, 70–71,
        236–37
cymbidium, 230–31, 260–61

dahlias, 68–69
daisies, 112–15
deli flowers
    deconstructing bouquet
        of, 65–67, 121
    upgrading, 155–63
    using roses from, 88–89
delphinium, 264–65
    water level for, 46
dome-shaped arrangement,
    89, 158–61, 242–43
dried flowers, 116–19
    hydrangeas, 46

eggs, 34–37
elephant ears, 204–5
elevated arrangements,
    98–107, 186–93
    boxes, 110–11
    cake stands, 54–55, 232,
        250–51
    high/low, 214–57
    See also books; pedestals
English garden roses, 22, 93
    advantages of, 235
    ceramic vase/cake stand
        arrangement, 250–51
    pink and chartreuse,
        108–11, 130–31
    single-stem arrangement,
        234–35
    yellow, 16–17
eremurus stems, 188–89

fan palms, 175, 176
ferns, 38–39, 179, 181, 257,
    275

fiddlehead, 96–97
floating arrangements,
    40–41, 50–51
flowers, 155–67
    decorating with, 182–83
    extending life of, 13, 46–47
    feeding of, 13
    fruit mixed with, 183
    garlands of, 63
    opening of, 46, 47
    places in house for, 274–75
    preparing, 13
    tools and materials,
        276–79
    See also bouquet guide;
        specific flowers
foliage. See leaves
footed bowl, 164, 166–67,
    232–35
Fragonard, Jean-Honoré,
    164–67
French bouquet, 88–89,
    155–63
    definition of, 89, 155
French paintings, 165–67
French tulips, 28–29
    autumn, 80
    in boxes, 44–45, 48–49
    in footed bowl, 233, 234–35
    grapes, 48–49, 208, 210–11
    lemons and limes, 206–7
    mixed with flowers, 183

garlands, 208, 210–11,
    252–55
    draping on window,
        253–54
    of flowers,
        63
geranium
    leaves,
        164
gerberas,
    246–49
glass balls,
    208,
    210–11
glass cloche,
    40–41
glass cyl-
    inders,
    172–73,
    174
    paper-
        wrapped,
        70–71,
        236–37
glass pitcher,
    106–7
glass vases,
    148–49
    black, 160,
        162, 163
    colored,
        143,

158–63, 196–97
square, 126–27, 160, 162
tall, 188–89
See also *bottles; green glass*
gomphrena. See *pom-poms*
gourdlike vases, 52–53
grapes, 48–49, 208, 210–11
grasses, 30–31, 33, 35, 36, 178–80
green glass
bottles, 82–89
cake stand, 54–55
water pitcher, 105–7
greens
berry branches, 96–97, 192–95
as Christmas decoration, 252, 257
climbing vine, 56–57
in colorful plastic bags, 38–39
elephant ears, 204–5
See also *garlands; leaves*

height. See *elevated arrangements*
heirlooms, 217
heliconias, hanging, 196–97
herbs, 82–89. See also *specific herbs*
high/low arrangements, 214–57
hydrangeas, 104, 106, 124–25, 186–87, 242–43
in paper-wrapped cylinder, 236–37
preserving, 46
smashing stem, 13

iris, 67
ivy, 56–57

Japanese motif, 48–51, 70–71

Kangaroo Paws, 202–3
knickknacks, 22–23

lady's mantle, 175, 177
lavender (color), 104–7, 126–27, 142, 228–29
old bottles, 235
vase, 162, 163
lavender (herb), 116–19
leaves, 59, 164, 206–7
green berry viburnum, 192–95
palm, 176, 176
removing from flower stem, 13, 238
silver, 134–35
tropical, 204–5
lemons and limes, 206–7
lilacs, 105–7, 238–39
lilies, 60–61, 264–65, 266–67
lysimachia, 134–35

Mahogany sunflowers, 149
maple leaves, 59
metal buckets, 65
metal sun sculpture, 126–27
milk glass cake stands, 54–55
mint stems, 82–89, 99, 164, 165
misting flowers, 13
moss, 19, 30, 35, 77
mugs. See *coffee mugs*

oasis blocks, uses for, 279
orchids, 19, 80, 138–41, 226–27
advantages of, 227
in bamboo steamer, 77, 79
in birdcage, 56–57
in colored bottles, 80–81, 244–45
contrasting, 260–61
egg arrangement, 34–37
floating in bowls, 50–51
mixed hot colors/heights, 193
planted, 228–29
re-hydrating, 46
in teacups, 30–33
ostrich eggs, 34–37

paint cans, 92–93
paintings. See *artworks*
palm leaves, 175, 176
paper
coffee cups, 24–26
gift-wrap, 118–19
-wrapped glass containers, 70–71, 236–37
paperwhites, 274
papyrus stems, 172–73, 174
pedestals, 198, 200–201, 274. See also *elevated arrangements*
pennies (in vessel water), 13
peonies, 22–23, 35, 40–41
in bud vases, 72–75
in ceramic vase, 132–33
in coffeepot, 214–15
in cupcake holders, 150–53
floating, 40–41
in glass cloche, 40–41
in gourdlike vases, 52, 53
in high/low arrangement, 238–39, 258–59
method for opening, 46
in paint cans, 92–93
pink/hot pink, 16–17, 90–91, 99, 106–7, 216–17, 262–63
red, 93
in salsa jar, 16–17
in shopping bag, 90–91
silk, 136–37
in trash can, 220–21

in watering can, 112–15
white, 16–17, 26, 40, 93, 112–15
yellow, 222–23
phalaenopsis, 50–51, 260–61
pine garlands, 208, 210–11, 252–55
pitchers, 106–7, 124–25
plastic bags, 38–39
pom-poms, 116–19, 128–31, 154–63, 170–71, 224–25
bronze, 148–49
green carnations, 27, 158–61
Kermit green, 130–31
poppies, 30–39
opening method, 46
pots, 35, 37, 116–19
purple, 126–27, 142, 228–29
flower shape/texture contrasts, 258–59
green mix, 104–7
See also *lavender*

rabbit ornament, 22–23
ranunculuses, 136–37
red motif, 268–69
rosemary stems, 82–89, 112–15
roses, 35, 58–59, 74–75
bouquet arrangement, 88–89, 93, 218
care of, 47
dome with hydrangeas, 242–43
opening, 46
orange and red clumps, 120–21
preparing, 13
pulling apart, 111
water for, 47
See also *English garden roses*
row arrangements, 28–29, 82–89, 128–29
rudbeckias, 148–49

salsa jars, 16–17
scabiosa, 112–15, 134–35, 164, 165
scale, 183, 200, 202
combination of, 243
scissors
gold and pink, 278
overscaled, 277
7UP (in vessel water), 13
shopping bags, 90–91
silk flowers, 136–37
silver, 65, 128–29, 224–25
trash cans, 218–21
silver leaves, 134–35
sneakers (as vessel), 42
soup tureen, 94–95, 120–21
Sprite (in vessel water), 13
steamer, 76–79

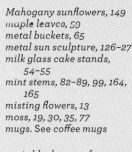

stems
   cutting, 13
    smashing, 13, 185, 238
    submerging, 13
succulents, 19–21
sunflowers, 144–49
supermarket flowers. See
   deli flowers
sweet peas, 258–59
sweet william, 42–43

take-out containers, 122–23
tall arrangements. See
   elevated arrangements
tea canisters, 17
teacups, 30–33
teapots, 214–17
terra-cotta pots, 35, 37

thorn removal, 13
three-dimensional effect,
   218, 273
tools and materials, 276–79
trash cans, 218–21
tree trunk, 208, 210–11
tropical leaves, 204–5
tulips, 28–29
turquoise vessels, 89,
   124–25, 132–33, 138–39,
   146–47, 250–51

urn, classical, 194–96

vanda orchids, 138–39
Van Gogh sunflowers,
   144–47

Venice glass, 232
vessels. See specific types
viburnum, green berry,
   192–95
vines, 56–57

water
   bacteria prevention, 13
   changing, 13
   level of, 46, 47
   oasis block soaking, 279
   room temperature, 13
   for specific flowers, 46–47
watercooler, 204, 205
water glass, 54–55, 90, 238
watering can, 112–15
water lilies, opening, 47
water pitchers, 105–7, 124–25

water tubes, uses for, 276
wheatgrass, 30–31, 33, 35, 36
White King Protea, 70–71
white vases and balls, 208,
   210–11
wildflowers, 113
wire, 278
wooden fruit boxes, 44–45
wooden vase, 161, 163
wrapping paper, 236

yellow James Storey
   orchids, 140–41
yellow theme, 222–23

"Zig Zag Pots," 151